What Industry Leaders Are Saying About
Zero to a Billion: 61 Rules Entrepreneurs Need to Know to Grow a Government Contracting Business

"I've known David Kriegman as an outstanding manager and leader, both at SRA and afterwards. His book, Zero to a Billion, is loaded with great ideas or 'rules' that are practical, sensible, and based on real life experience. I highly recommend it to every manager, not only new or mid-career executives but also anyone who has been in business for a while and is still open to new ideas. David has written a value-packed book that's a must read."

Renny DiPentima
Former President and CEO of SRA International

"*Zero to a Billion* explains why some companies succeed and some don't. David uses his experience to present easy-to-follow rules for growing and managing a successful company.

Each rule is illustrated with real-world examples that bring the rule to life. Anyone who wants to take their company to the next level needs to read this book. It should be on every manager's reading list."

Duane Andrews, Former CEO, QinetiQ North America
Former COO, SAIC
Former Assistant Secretary of Defense (C3I)
and Chief Information Officer

"Doing business with the federal government means having to comply with a bookshelf full of laws, regulations, directives and agency practices. Almost all of them dictate how to be a **compliant** government contractor. Nowhere in that minefield are there techniques to be a successful government contractor. Dave Kriegman's three core principles and 61 rules provide business leaders with actionable steps to be that successful federal professional services contractor. You should hope your competitors aren't reading this, too."

Alan Chvotkin, Esq.
Professional Services Council

"David has written an insightful guide to building a successful federal services company, both winning approaches and some to avoid, all based on his decades of relevant personal experiences at companies large and small; a primer speaking to the importance of awareness for all senior mangers to keep top of mind as they build their businesses."

Peter Schulte, Founder and Managing Partner, CM Equity Partners.

"This is a guidebook that captures the fundamental rules for success in this business. More than a "must-read" book for managers in the world of government contracting, it also serves as a reference book and scorecard that should be consulted on an on-going basis. I wish I had it years ago. I would have purchased and distributed copies for my entire management and business development teams.

The book is easy to read with plenty of real world examples that bring the lessons to life. I strongly encourage readers to heed this advice."

Mike Stolarik
Former President and COO of QinetiQ North America
and Analex Corporation
Former CEO, Space Applications Corporation
and GRC International
Former Corporate Vice President, BDM International

"*Zero to a Billion* is a quick read with easy to understand, essential lessons not often found in the business books I've read. David has years and years of practical experience doing business with the United States government. Now smart entrepreneurs can leverage that experience, distilled into 61 Rules, to successfully grow a government contracting business."

Steven H. Weiss
Executive Vice President
Government Business Operations
Corporate Ombudsman, CACI

"Unlike management science books written by academics and filled with little more than congealed common sense, David brings the perspectives of an in-the-trenches practitioner and leader whose views have been shaped by hard-earned lessons learned. David has a keen appreciation for the value – and fragility – of a company culture and why so many good companies lost their footing and what they need to do to regain it.

The ultimate value of David's 61 rules is not gleaned from reading them, but rather from practicing them. Only then will you appreciate what differentiates the best companies from the lucky companies, and the most successful innovators from the legions of 'me too' self-proclaimed entrepreneurs. Finally, a book that speaks to middle and senior management in actionable terms – a true *tour de force* from an insider in the Government contracting sector."

Barry S. Landew
Founder and Managing Director, Wolf Den Associates
Former SRA International Executive

"During the last two years, David has been an indispensible part of our success. Through the practical application of his 61 Rules, and his steady guidance and counsel, we have more than doubled. We have benefited from his practical, applicable rules and advice concerning strategy, business development, and execution. He has added tremendous value as a consultant and member of our Board of Advisers, and we are grateful for his participation!"

Steven Flannery, CEO, The RSR Company

"Every company (large or small, new or established) doing business in the Federal market space faces enormous challenges and abundant opportunities to succeed and grow in today's market climate. David Kriegman's '61 Rules' are relevant, timely, useful guidance to new **entrepreneurs** and seasoned executives. More importantly, it challenges business owners and executives to think strategically about their objectives, their value proposition, their service delivery, and their people. Successful people understand that life is about learning and the '61 Rules' is a great desk-side companion for those who seek to continuously learn so they can grow their business, delight their customers and care for their employees."

Bill Donahue, Lt Gen USAF (Retired)

"*Zero to a Billion* conveys strategies and tactics for success at any business. It is a treasure trove of invaluable lessons, some of which can be applied immediately and many over a long-term. When business owners/managers are cognizant of its lessons, the book provides a guide for enhancing their business with even minimal implementation."

Adam August, Partner,
Holland & Knight LLP

"David Kriegman's book is a must read for any entrepreneur or management team trying to succeed in today's business world, especially in the federal sector. His insights pertaining to everything from the importance of adapting to paradigm shifts in the market to the need to play everyone in the customer's organization man on man are valuable, accurate and astute. David's experience helping to propel SRA, as well as the other companies he has championed, into the stratosphere of success have provided him and now the reader with an essential play book of how to succeed in business."

Courtney Banks Spaeth
CEO, NSAWW

"David delivers rare insight regarding what it takes to become a proven leader in the world of government contracting. A fascinating tale about how a leadership team's corporate culture can become a pivotal part of the entire organization's continued success."

JD Kathuria, CEO & Founder of WashingtonExec

"Unlike most business memoirs, the protagonist in David's book is the reader, not the author. This is a how-to text that transcends stale academic case studies by bringing a 'been there, done that' practitioner's perspective to address a myriad of growth company challenges.

SRA established the gold standard for organic growth in the federal sector – with many years of consecutive, sustained, double-digit growth across federal civilian, health, defense, intelligence, and homeland security markets. This book codifies many of the business rules that enabled that great run in an intuitive format that should serve as an owner's manual for anyone to grow their federal business."

Kevin Robbins
Managing Director, Wolf Den Associates
Co-founder, BlueDelta Capital Partners

"David Kriegman's chapter, 'Talent Management,' in his book *Zero to A Billion* presents nine critical, concise, and common-sense tips on how to most effectively utilize a company's talent for maximum benefit for both the company and the staff."

Stanley L. Krejci
Principal, The SK Group, LLC

"One of the most difficult challenges every Founder/CEO faces is guiding a business from start-up through the numerous challenges of growth. David is one of those rare individuals who helped build a small business to revenues greater than $1B. Having worked with David and others at SRA, I saw first-hand the way the team adapted to growth, made tough decisions and created one of the best companies to work for in America.

Embrace this book and learn first-hand from an executive who experienced it all. Perhaps it will help you avoid the many land mines along the way as you build your business."

Evan Scott, CEO, ESGI
Executive Search Consultants to Federal Contractors.

To Chad,
All the Best.
David Finnegan

Zero to a Billion

ZERO TO A BILLION

61 Rules Entrepreneurs Need to Know to Grow a Government Contracting Business

David Kriegman,
former Chief Operating Officer
SRA International

DUDLEY COURT PRESS

Dedication

To my wife, Suzan Zimmerman, the best business development person in the industry. This book would not have been completed without her support. Her suggestions and guidance over the years are the foundation on which this book was written.

Published in the United States of America by:
Dudley Court Press, LLC
PO Box 102
Sonoita, AZ 85637
www.DudleyCourtPress.com

Cover and Interior Design: M. Urgo
Stamp image: iStockphoto

LCCN: 2013949052
ISBN: 978-1-940013-04-6 (paper)
978-1-940013-03-9 (hardcover)
978-1-940013-05-3 (epub)

Publisher's Cataloging-in-Publication Data:

Kriegman, David A., 1946-
    Zero to a billion : 61 rules entrepreneurs need to know to grow a government contracting business / by David Kriegman.—Sonoita, AZ : Dudley Court Press, c2013.

    p. ; cm.

    ISBN: 978-1-940013-04-6 (paper) ; 978-1-940013-03-9 (hardcover) ; 978-1-940013-05-3 (epub)
    Includes index.
    Summary: A practical, how-to guide for entrepreneurs who want to build a successful government contracting business. Former SRA International executive David Kriegman draws on his thirty years of experience to illustrate the essential lessons of strategy, business development, cultural issues and operations with real-world examples and actionable ideas. The book is recommended for new and mid-career managers as well as seasoned executives.--Publisher.

    1. Entrepreneurship--Handbooks, manuals, etc. 2. Government contractors--United States--Handbooks, manuals, etc. 3. Consultants--United States–Handbooks, manuals, etc. 4. Knowledge workers–United States–Handbooks, manuals, etc. 5. Professional corporations--United States–Handbooks, manuals, etc. 6. Public contracts–United States. 7. Success in business. 8. Business planning. 9. Leadership. 10. Management science. I. Title. II. Title: Sixty-one rules entrepreneurs need to know to grow a government contracting business.

    HB615 ..K75 2013   2013949052
    658.4/21--dc23   1311

To engage with David Kriegman, please visit his website: www.Z2B-LLC.com

Contents

Foreword

I've learned that as an entrepreneur, the degree to which I communicate and collaborate with my customers is a leading indicator of how successful I've been. I've also found that when you do that in the government marketplace, it gets you thrown in jail.

So stated the founder of a small business in testimony to the United States Senate twenty years ago. His statement, delivered at a hearing on major overhauls to federal acquisition rules and processes, was intended to highlight one simple, usually obvious, but often overlooked fact: the government is a unique customer that, while relying on the commercial market for goods and services, behaves unlike any other customer in that market. Government procurement is dominated and driven by a set of rules and often conflicting objectives, and, of course, the sometimes knee-jerk reactions of the body politic. It is also the only market in which the "customer" often has no control over the business relationship. That is, the government operates on the foundation of "actual authority," meaning that ONLY a warranted government contracting officer can commit government funds and/or enter into a contract. Yet those contracting officers are not generally the customer; in fact, in many cases, they are actually significantly distanced from the true customer, the part of the organization that will actually utilize and capitalize on the offered goods or services.

For these reasons and more, some, indeed many, entrepreneurs have opted to simply avoid the federal marketplace. Yet, many others have jumped in with both feet and often succeeded, not just as a business, but as a provider of services critical to the right functioning of the government and the security of the nation.

Today, the federal government procures more than $325 billion in services alone each and every year. Every type of service imaginable, from information technology and engineering to maintenance and repair; from social science and research services to logistics, management consulting, data analytics, international development and much more. It is also a dynamic market that has undergone tectonic shifts over the last two decades and may well be on the cusp of yet another significant adjustment. Each of these changes has confirmed one seemingly counter-intuitive characteristic of the government: despite its glacial pace and sometimes overwhelmingly bureaucratic nature, the government market is also Darwinian; change DOES happen and those who survive and thrive amidst that change are those that adapt most effectively and quickly.

For example, in the mid-1990s, the majority of services procured by the government were bought individually, on stand-alone contracts. By the mid-2000s, 70% or more of those procurements were done on a more incremental basis, through task orders awarded to companies that had been pre-qualified by "winning" a spot on a larger, master contract known as a "multiple award." This shift completely changed the competitive landscape and the costs of doing business with the government. Instead of developing one bid for work, companies now often have to invest in a bid to win "a place" on the multiple award vehicle and then again invest in bidding for individual task orders through which the real work—and revenue—flows.

Another major shift occurred in the aftermath of 9/11. Among the other impacts of that horrific event was the recognition of a new and daunting set of security requirements—facility, personal, systems, national—for which we were simply not prepared. The cost of the wars in Iraq and Afghanistan aside, federal spending on high end professional and technology services skyrocketed. Entirely new and/or radically restructured institutional infrastructure was put into place, including both the Department of Homeland Security and the coalescing of numerous intelligence assets under the at least partial direction and control of a new Director of National Intelligence. From 2002 to about 2009, spending on professional and technology services grew every year, sometimes by double digits and always at a rate faster than the overall federal budget, which itself was on a steady upward path.

By 2010, however, the sands again began to shift and yet a new paradigm began to emerge. That paradigm is actually a combination of forces, including reduced spending and resources, a government human capital crisis that remains largely unaddressed and unabated, and the still increasingly rapid pace of technology change. For companies in the government market, these changes have required substantial adjustments, from talent management and workforce "greening" strategies, to dramatic reductions in overhead costs, increased competition for talent, growing compliance costs, and margin pressures. All of this is coming at a time when industry itself is undergoing a major transformation as new technologies, including but not limited to cloud, virtual servers, and more, are fundamentally changing business models and go to market strategies and offerings. To put it mildly, today's federal market is not for the faint of heart.

So why would any entrepreneur want to be in this market? The answer is both simple and complex. The simplest reason, and one that continues to motivate many, is the mission itself. Beyond that, the government is still a good customer, a big customer, and, for the most part, a fair customer. But understanding the complex rules and compliance regimes, the unique structures of authority, funding, and interplay of business and socio-economic rules and objectives are essential. The entrepreneur seeking to lead a company into this market must understand how and why some new entries have succeeded where so many others have failed; must understand how one can—and cannot—build the kinds of business relationships and capabilities that lead to successful engagements; and must recognize how and when to invest in internal capacity, personnel and infrastructure so the company is effectively positioned to prosper and grow.

For those of us with far less insight and expertise than David Kriegman, the rules of thumb seem simple: be agile, be customer focused, think ahead, and be realistic. Easy rules indeed. But as with any business, moving from concept to execution is the key. And "Zero to a Billion" is designed to help you do just that. In this book, David Kriegman sets forth a set of rules that are really a thinker's guideposts. Some of them break with conventional wisdom; others help explain why some tried and true formulas still work. Nothing can prepare you for the experience of the government market, but "Zero to a Billion" can and will help take some of the mystery out of what it really takes to be successful.

Over the last two decades, it has become clear that the future of the government's ability to effectively execute its many and varied missions is going to increasingly rely on its ability to effectively partner with the private sector. Workforce age and skills imbalances, compensation pressures, and the pace of change taking place outside of government have all converged to fundamentally change the way in which the government delivers. Resource constraints notwithstanding, that trend will continue for the foreseeable future. The challenges are real. So too are the opportunities. David Kriegman's book is a major contribution to ensuring the government services contractors will be up to the job.

Stan Soloway
President and CEO, Professional Services Council
Former Deputy Undersecretary of Defense

Acknowledgements

I had the good fortune to work with many people from many companies, and I learned something from everyone. I can't thank everyone who deserves an acknowledgement, but I would like to recognize several people who taught me the lessons in this book. Many of the rules in this book came from Ted Legasey, and he deserves a lot of the credit for this book. Ted was the first person that Ernst Volgeneau hired when he started SRA, and Ted served as SRA's COO for most of the time I was there. Ted was the day-to-day face of the company to the employees and led the implementation of SRA's values and its culture. Ernst Volgeneau was the entrepreneur who had the vision to establish SRA as one of the best companies in the world. I can't thank Ernst enough for creating a company that taught me so much. Emerson Thompson was the person who hired me into SRA. He was my boss, mentor, and friend and made several suggestions that made this a better book. Renny DiPentima led SRA's business for the federal government and became SRA's CEO. After a distinguished career as a senior executive in government, Renny adapted perfectly to the world of government contracting. Many of the rules in this book are a result of discussions he and I had over the years. Barry Landew and Jeff (JR) Rydant are the two most creative proposal writers in the business. We would not have won many of the jobs described in this book without their leadership and creative ideas. Barry, together with his partner, Kevin Robbins, now lead the consulting company Wolf Den Associates. Barry and Kevin both contributed directly to this book. Barry helped clarify some of the examples from SRA's early days, and Kevin made significant contributions to the section on Mergers and Acquisitions. Gary Nelson graciously let me use one his secrets for getting the staff to focus on large jobs. Gary was responsible for business development when I joined SRA, and he helped orient my mind to focus on customers. I'd like to thank Wayne Blackburn, who

Acknowledgements

was deputy director of Defense Systems while I was the director. Wayne deserves a lot credit for the success of the business and the development of my thought processes. Suzan Zimmerman suggested some of rules associated with business development. Suzan was responsible for many of the largest wins at one of the major federal contractors. She is now Senior Vice President for Strategic Capture at CACI. I would like to thank Izzy Feldman for his early guidance and encouragement when the book was still in the early stages of development. I would also like to thank Jake Zimmerman and Max Chernoff for providing a youthful perspective.

I am greatly indebted to my editor, writing coach, and publisher, Gail Woodard of Dudley Court Press. Gail's suggestions throughout the writing and publishing process were invaluable. My copy editor, Robert Juran, was extremely helpful during the editing process.

Most of all, I would like to thank the men and women, in and out of uniform, who serve our government. Working with these dedicated public servants has made my career worthwhile and fulfilling.

David Kriegman
August, 2013

Introduction

I am fortunate to have worked with companies at all stages of growth. I worked with companies of all sizes from start-up companies to companies with revenue of more than a billion dollars. I spent 23 years at SRA International, Inc. where I experienced growth from being small to being a billion-dollar company. After leaving SRA, I worked with a start-up company, a publicly traded commercial company that was moving into government services, and a large global company. In my current consulting practice, I am advising companies whose revenues ranges from $2.5M a year to over a billion dollars a year. Along the way, I have worked alongside many other companies of all sizes.

I was fortunate to work for SRA from its early days, through the period when it became a public company and revenues exceeded a billion dollars. For several decades, SRA International, Inc. was one of the most admired companies in the government professional services industry. The company was started in Ernst Volgeneau's basement and quickly established a reputation for aggressive growth and honest service. For nine years, SRA was recognized by Fortune magazine as one of the 100 Best Companies to Work For and by Washingtonian magazine as one of the Best Places to Work in the D.C. Area. SRA went public in 2002 and enjoyed a positive relationship with Wall Street analysts and investors. It was admired by many of the other companies in the field. During my tenure at SRA I met many small and mid-sized companies whose officers told me that they were trying to emulate SRA and its success. I was frequently asked to speak to the leaders of these small companies on what made us so successful.

SRA enjoyed a reputation for winning a higher-than-average percentage of the proposals that they submitted to the government. One customer remarked to me that SRA's reputation was that SRA would submit a proposal only on jobs that they expected to win. That wasn't quite true, but it does illustrate the reputation that SRA enjoyed in the community.

I joined SRA in 1983 after working for the government for seven years. I was hired by SRA to work on a new $7.6M contract for the architecture and design of a modernized command and control system for the Army. Prior to winning that contract, SRA's annual revenue was only $4.8M. Over the course of the next twenty years, I helped grow and manage SRA's business. I was director of Army Programs when we became a leader in developing information technology systems for the Army in the mid-1990s. I became the director of Defense Systems in 1997 when the revenue in that business unit was $47M. Over the next seven years, we grew the defense business to over $400M in annual revenue. SRA's stock was listed on the New York Stock exchange in 2002. I became Chief Operating Officer in 2004 and focused on taking care of employees across the company, operations across the entire company, and acquisitions. While I was COO, we acquired Galaxy International, the Touchstone Consulting Group, Spectrum Corporation, and Mercomms Unlimited, Inc. I led the integration of these companies into SRA.

After I left SRA, I was the president of two smaller companies. The first was an investor-backed start-up company, Command Information, focused on the next generation of the Internet. The second company, Tech Team Government Solutions, Inc., was a wholly owned subsidiary of a publicly traded global IT company, Tech Team Global. We sold Tech Team Government Solutions to a very large global technology and engineering company. That sale gave me experience in selling a company, and I was then able to experience the integration of an acquired company from the other side. After the integration was completed, I formed a consulting firm, Z2B, LLC, to help companies achieve their strategic goals.

Over the course of the last 30 years, I compiled a set of lessons that cover all aspects of growing and operating businesses of all sizes. These lessons emerged from what we did right, what we did wrong, and what I observed from working with many companies throughout the years and in my current consulting practice. Presented here in the form of rules, these lessons provide proven ways to help you achieve your strategic growth objectives. By studying these rules, you will learn both general principles and specific techniques that will help you answer some of the key questions that all businesses face.

1. Why do some companies grow while others stagnate or go out of business?

2. How do you differentiate yourself as a services company?

3. How do you compete with much larger companies?

4. Why do you lose work when the customer says you are doing a good job?

5. Why are some companies able to deliver systems on time while others are habitually late?

6. How do you scale your business efficiently as you grow?

7. How do you attract, retain, and motivate top talent?

8. Why do some acquisitions succeed while others are considered less than a success or even a failure?

9. How do you position your company for the next stage, whether it is a sale, going public, or becoming an enduring private enterprise such as an employee-owned company?

Along with each rule, I present real-world examples of how I have seen that rule applied. Most of the examples are from the professional services industry that supports the federal government. However, many of these examples apply to service providers in other industries as well.

This book also explains some general, unifying principles that leaders of companies will find valuable as they define what differentiates their company from their competitors. There are a few principles from which almost all of the rules can be derived.

For organizational purposes, the rules are grouped into the following areas: Strategy, Business Development, Operations, Talent Management, and the integration of Mergers and Acquisitions. However, in the business world, strategy, business development, and even operations are so closely linked that you shouldn't take the divisions as absolute. Like many companies in their formative years, in the early days of SRA we made a point of "everyone sells," so we tried to integrate operations and business development/growth as much as possible.

There is not a one-to-one correspondence between the rules and the nine questions above. Questions 1 and 2 are broad questions and several of the rules in the Strategy and Business Development sections address them, but rules 1 and 2 are especially on point. You will find approaches to addressing Question 3 among many of the rules in the first two parts, but rules 4, 12, and 23 address this question specifically. Rules 16, 20, 22, and 24 also contain some specific advice to address this question. Question 4 is one that companies are facing at a greater rate than ever before. Again, you will find a lot of advice throughout the book to help with this, but you should pay particular attention to rules 4, 34, 38, 39, 45, and 54. Rules 35, 40, and 43 are especially important to answering Question 5. Question 6 deals with internal operations and organization. Pay attention to the rules in Part 3, especially 36, 38, 41, 42, and 44. Question 7 is about people/talent management. While Part 4 addresses this question specifically, keep in mind that a service business is a people business and following the rules in Part 4 affect all aspects of growing and operating a successful business. Question 8 asks how to make your acquisitions successful. Part 5 is designed to present real-world advice in this area. Question 9 is an overall strategy question that goes to the heart of your strategy, vision, and culture. You will find that most of the rules in Part 1 will help you find your answer.

PART ONE
STRATEGY

1. Be known for something

Many companies, in their early years, haven't defined a focus for themselves. They may have started by securing a contract to perform a certain type of work, but they haven't made a decision to specialize in that or any other specific area. They are interested in growing their business, and they don't care where the revenue comes from. A desire to grow is not a strategy. It is especially important for small businesses to understand that they have to be known for something.

I've met many small-business leaders who, when I ask what they do, say, "We do everything; we are a mini-SRA." They were saying that they didn't care what kind of work I offered them. They just wanted more revenue, but they couldn't give me any reason why I should select them over the thousands of other companies that could perform the same services. When you are small, you have to be known for at least one specialty. There has to be some specific reason for a customer to want you or for a prime contractor to want you on their team. That specialty can be a technical specialty such as expertise in a specific product or a functional specialty such as logistics or personnel. It can also be relationships with or a deep knowledge of a specific customer. There has to be some focus to your growth strategy and positioning.

Some small businesses do start out with a focus. Usually these are companies with a strong functional background. That is, the founders come out of a government agency and are providing non-technical services back to that or similar agencies. Those companies usually have a value proposition that they can articulate to a customer or potential prime contractor when they are looking to obtain a subcontractor role on a large project. Even in this case, the company needs to define that value proposition.

It can be "Hire us because we are the experts in logistics," or "Hire us because we understand how the Diplomatic Security office at the Department of State operates and what they need."

Technical companies have a more difficult time defining their value proposition. A company that starts out by managing computer networks or doing general software development has a more difficult time expressing why it is different from its competitors. There are some companies that have made a name for themselves by concentrating on a single technology or product. For example, there are small business who specialize in supporting Microsoft SharePoint. These companies are limited in what they do (as I'll explain in the next rule), but at least they have a value proposition that gives someone a reason to hire them.

As a small business, a value proposition that says, "Hire us because we are the best at xxxx" has a lot of marketing strength. If you really are that good at some functional or technical area, then prime contractors will want you on their team, and government customers will want your service. This business model has a lot of advantages. You have something different to offer, your services may be worth more on an hourly basis than your competitors, and you probably will not use subcontractors, which will help your financials.

As you grow, there is a downside to a business model that relies solely on specialties. You will rarely be the prime contractor on large jobs, and therefore there will be a limit to how large you can become. Rule 2 will discuss how to address this downside.

2. Become a systems integrator

If you want to grow to a billion dollars, you have to understand the value proposition of a systems integrator. There are two types of companies in the government professional services business: niche specialty companies and solution providers. Solution providers are sometimes referred to as systems integrators. For this discussion, I will use those terms interchangeably. I have worked with specialty companies that focus on functional specialties such as logistics and technical specialties such as Microsoft products (e.g., Sharepoint), business intelligence products, information assurance, or enterprise resource planning (ERP) systems. Solution providers approach customer problems from a different perspective that I'll describe in this section. The differences between these two types of companies are described in the table below:

Specialty Companies	System Integrators
Value Proposition: Best technical or functional in their specialty	Value Proposition: Best value for a total solution
Focus on what they do well	Focus on the customer's problem. Will do whatever it takes to make the customer successful
Focus is on the technology	Focus is on applying the technology to solve a specific customer problem
High labor component	Emphasis on system level activities and selected other activities
Little or no use of subs	Uses subs for appropriate parts of the job
Relatively high rates	Develops a set of competitive rate structures
Rarely primes large jobs	Primes large, complex jobs

You may not think of yourself as being in the systems integration business, but if you want to grow to be large, you need to be thinking about yourself as a solutions provider/systems integrator. Unless the market for your niche service is very large, your growth will come from solving your customers' broader problems.

There was a lot of discussion within SRA over the years about our growth strategy. Many people within SRA saw us as a niche specialty company without understanding the ramifications. When I joined SRA in 1983, we were known for our functional and analytical expertise. In the early 1980s, SRA was responsible for defining the requirements for the modernized Army World Wide Military Command and Control System. When it came time for the government to implement that system, some folks at SRA didn't think that we should get into the business of software or systems development. They argued that we should leave that "low end" work to others. They didn't have a vision of how to grow. Perhaps they wanted SRA to stay a small boutique firm and not grow to be a large company. They didn't understand that they were limiting our potential.

Being known for only a small number of specialties limits growth. Sometimes people will think that being known as a specialty company is a means of growing. When the Internet and Web came into being, some leaders thought that the SRA brand should stand for Web development. They didn't understand that a company's brand needs to stand for something that doesn't change, especially something that doesn't change as rapidly as technology changes.

There isn't anything wrong with being a specialty company or being known only for a technical or functional specialty. This strategy becomes questionable only if you desire to become a large company.

If you want to become a large company, you need to become a prime contractor on large jobs. Specialty companies rarely prime large jobs. Contracts that ask only for a specialty service are not sufficiently large to enable you to grow to be very large. SRA was known for several specialties. Among those were natural language processing and data mining. Both of these specialties were very important to our growth and the image of high-end services that we wanted to project. However, no project in these areas would ever bring in more than a few hundred thousand dollars. If we were going to grow to a billion dollars, we needed contracts in the millions of dollars a year. Specialty companies are not prepared to undertake these large jobs. I'll describe an example from the early 1990s when SRA's revenue was around $50M.

We had a contract with the Army Information Systems Software Center. The Army had a need to develop a new system. At the time, Object Oriented Development was the big buzzword and technique for software development. A small company sold the Army on its ability to do Object Oriented Design and Development. The Army informed it that we held the software development contract so that they had to work with us. The senior people from that company approached us and said that on this job, even though we held the prime contract, they should act as the "prime" and the lead for this development. SRA could pick up the ongoing operations and maintenance after the system was developed. I said, "Fine, but I have a few questions. Who will be responsible for specifying and developing the interfaces to the other Army systems that this system will have to interface with?" They said that SRA should do that, since they just do Object Oriented development and we had expertise in the Army systems. I then asked, "Who will size the hardware requirements, since this will require new hardware?" Again they said that SRA should. I said, "Who will look at the load on the network to see if we were allocated suitable bandwidth?" "Who will be responsible for training the users?" After several of these questions, they just said, "Maybe SRA should be the lead and we should just be responsible for the Object Oriented Design."

It was around this time that the Web was becoming prominent, and it was becoming clear that all new development would eventually work through the Web. I was encouraged to present myself to my customer, the Army, as its web developer. Like the exchange about Object Oriented development, I said that if I tried to sell us that way to this customer, the likely response would be, "That's nice. Go see EDS. They are my systems integrator."

That led me to wonder, "What is a systems integrator? What makes a good systems integrator?" Rule 3 answers those questions.

3. Excel in three areas

At SRA, we thought for some time that systems integrators were the developers of a system. That isn't true. The Information Technology Association of America (ITAA) developed a definition of systems integration in 1987. According to ITAA, systems integration is *a process by which multiple products and services are identified and assembled into a* **complete solution** *to a* **complex** *information system or sub-system requirement.*

Systems integrators may be responsible for many aspects of a project, including:

Architecture and Design
Detailed Design
Project Management
Systems Engineering
System and Applications Software Engineering
Hardware & Software Design/Implementation
Make/Buy Decisions
Procurement
Subcontract Management
Financing
Assembly and Testing
Deployment
Logistic Support
Network Operations
Facility Operations
Maintenance
Training

There are only three of these activities that the Systems Integrator MUST provide and MUST be expert at. These are: **Project Management, Systems Engineering**, and **Subcontract Management**. Everything else can be assigned to subcontractors to perform, but these three activities must be performed by the prime contractor.

At SRA, this was a hard lesson to learn. When I first briefed this to SRA leaders, a light went on. Every time we gave systems engineering work to a subcontractor, we subsequently lost that work to that subcontractor. When SRA won a very large contract to modernize the Command and Control system for the Department of Defense (what became GCCS-Joint), we decided to keep the software development for ourselves and assign the systems engineering role to our subcontractor, SAIC, which had no previous experience with either the system or the customer, the Defense Information Systems Agency, DISA. This made sense to us, since the systems engineering group was much smaller than the software development group. When the follow-on contract was being competed, DISA divided the work into two procurements. The first was called the DII/COE contract. This was a single award to build the infrastructure, called the Common Operating Environment (COE). The second was a multiple award contract to build the applications on top of this infrastructure. The DII/COE contract was the jewel, and SRA bid that as a prime contractor. DISA, however, saw SAIC as the systems integrator and they won that contract. SRA was viewed as the software developer, but we chose to bid that contract as a subcontractor, figuring we couldn't win both as a prime. So we were relegated to being a subcontractor on a multiple award contract and having to compete for each of the applications. Eventually we lost that work to lower-priced small businesses. We learned a hard lesson: **Never sub out the systems engineering work**.

Equally important is to recognize the importance of project management and subcontract management as key corporate capabilities. It helps if there is a common, company-wide set of processes for project management in which everyone receives training. At SRA, we put a considerable amount of effort developing a week-long course in project management and made it a requirement for anyone in a leadership position on a project.

Niche companies can survive with a niche. However, they seldom grow to be a billion-dollar company. But doesn't a company need specialties to be able to penetrate new customers? Absolutely. Rule 1 says that when you are small, you can't present yourself as a systems integrator and effectively compete with expertise only in project management, systems engineering, and subcontractor management. Even a large systems integrator needs to be thought of as an expert in some areas. Maintaining the right balance between being a specialist and being a systems integrator is a key challenge for companies to address and a major theme of many of the rules in this book. Later rules will describe the role of specialties within a system integration company and how to be known for being both a systems integrator and for having specialized expertise in some areas. In every company, regardless of size, there is a natural tension between focusing on specialty offerings and focusing on customer needs. How a company chooses to deal with this tension affects how it will organize, how it will incentivize employees, and how it will go to market. It is necessary to learn how to capitalize on this tension and make it constructive tension rather than destructive tension.

4. Solve the customer's underlying problem

If there is a single piece of advice that every services company needs to learn, it is this: **Every time a customer asks you to do something, he or she has an underlying problem that needs to be solved.** Usually they haven't told you about that problem, and sometimes the customer may not even realize what it takes to be successful. The key to serving the customer and growing a business is to determine what that problem is and help the customer solve that problem. I have heard many business development folks say that the most important question to ask a customer is, "What keeps you up at night?" That is an important question, but it will not help you determine the underlying problem. The most important questions start with "Why," as in, "Why do you want this service?" "Why is it important to you?" Most companies focus only on what is asked for, but winners focus on solving the customer's underlying problem. (The idea of solving a customer's underlying problem comes from Fred Wiersema and Michael Treacy. The approach is described in their best-selling book, *The Discipline of Market Leaders* and other writings.) I'll present a simple way of thinking about this, and show how we applied it to a major service acquisition.

When I explain the concept of solving the customer's underlying problem, I often relate this story. Not long ago I had a case of influenza. I had all the symptoms: fever, headache, sore throat, sneezing. I was generally miserable. I went to my doctor and was given a prescription for an antibiotic. I took the prescription to my local pharmacy, which did just what I asked it to do: filled it promptly, accurately, and at a fair price. But the pharmacist missed an opportunity. She could have said something like this: "I see you have the flu. I can tell that by the prescription, and what I see—you're sneezing, coughing, you look miserable. This antibiotic will help, but it will take a few days to start to work. In the meantime, you will still feel miserable. But I have this cough medicine, which, if you take it now, will make you feel a little bit better until the antibiotic kicks in."

That's the classic up-sell approach. I'm suggesting that the pharmacist go even further. If she were observant, she might have said this: "I also see that you are having back problems. I'll bet that's from those shoes you are wearing. [I was still wearing my Earth Shoes from the 1970s.] I don't sell shoes, but I have an arrangement with the shoe store next door (my subcontractor). I'll set you up with them, and you will go home feeling much better right away." While I asked for the prescription to be filled, what I wanted was to feel better. The pharmacist should have focused on what she could do to make me feel better. Instead she focused on what I asked her to do.

It was by solving the customer's underlying problem that SRA won its first job with an initial contract value of over $300M.

CSC's contract for the U.S. Agency for International Development (USAID) was coming up for a re-competition around 2002. CSC was responsible for operations and maintenance of the USAID network worldwide and of some their back-office systems. The recompete procurement was for over six years and had an estimated value of over $300M. The draft Request for Proposals (RFP) read as if the government was looking for an outsourcing solution. The winning contractor would be responsible for running the worldwide networks under a set of Service Level Agreements (SLAs). The RFP was going to be released under a GSA multiple-award contract. The contract holders included CSC, EDS, Lockheed-Martin, BAH, SAIC, Northrop Grumman, Raytheon, and SRA. Our civil government sector looked at the draft RFP and said that there wasn't any way that SRA could beat EDS and the others in an outsourcing bid. We couldn't say that we can run a network better than EDS and CSC. The lead of another sector felt the same way. Renny DiPentima, President of SRA's federal business, and I both wanted to bid this. I was leading our Defense Sector at the time. While this was clearly a civil government job, we agreed to bid this. Renny said to me that we should propose Jon Hertzog as our Program Manager, but we had recently made Jon the Technical Lead on our recent win on the Reserve Component Automation System (RCAS). This job was worth over $100M, and we couldn't pull Jon off of that project so soon after the award. My response to Renny was: "Why, I'd rather propose myself than Jon." Renny quickly said, "Sold," so I became the PM.

So how were we going to beat CSC, EDS, SAIC, and the others on a $300M outsourcing job? At that time, SRA didn't even have much business running networks, let alone a job of this size. What we did have from our business development lead, Steve Flannery, was an understanding of the underlying problem of the USAID Information Resource Management (IRM) shop. The IRM office, like Chief Information Officer (CIO) offices across the government, wanted to get their arms around all of the IT work being done in the agency. At USAID, some of the IT development occurred at bureaus and missions around the world. If something went wrong, they asked IRM to fix it, but they didn't always go to IRM to develop the system in the first place. We knew that if we could persuade the IRM folks that we could help them serve their customers better, we could win this program.

Our proposal was led by Jeff (JR) Rydant, one the most creative minds in the business. JR understood that we didn't need to persuade the government that we could manage a network better than CSC, EDS, and the others. We needed only to persuade them that we could operate the network as well as the others. But in addition, we could do much more for them. We could help them solve their underlying problem and be more successful with their customers. Steve Flannery and JR devised a proposal around three stages: **Establish** IRM as a world-class provider of IT services, **Refresh** that capability with new technology over time, and **Add** additional capabilities so that IRM could serve their customers in more and better ways. Our proposal was organized around:

Establish, Refresh, Add, a New ERA for USAID

We walked into our oral presentation session wearing buttons declaring "A New **ERA** for USAID." We got the reaction that is needed every time you have orals. The goal is to walk out with the evaluation board saying to themselves, "That's the team I want!" We won the job, valued at $320M for over 6 years.

So you're probably asking, did we accomplish what we bid? Did we help IRM do more for their customers? Yes. Within a year, we expanded the contract to over $120M a year. The additional funds came from the bureaus that were IRM's customers, as they asked IRM to perform more services for them. We helped make IRM successful.

Sometimes the customer isn't even aware of what it needs to make itself successful. A couple of years ago we lost a job for one of the CIOs at the National Institutes of Health (NIH). At the debriefing, it appeared that our proposal scored high and we were low cost as well. I asked the CIO, "Why did we lose? How did the winning proposal rate?" He answered that the winning proposal said that they would help him, the CIO, decide where he should spend his money rather than just do what we were asked to do in the RFP. The CIO then said, "When I read that, I realized that that was what I really needed. If I had realized that sooner, I would have made it a requirement in the RFP." It is important to keep this in mind, not just for proposals, but for execution too. That brings me to my next lesson.

5. You can't choose what you do

I always generated some controversy when I would say, "You can choose your customers, but you can't choose what you do for them." I'll explain what I mean by this and why it was controversial within SRA.

First, it is important to realize that you do choose your customers, and one of the criteria for choosing is that they have the kind of work you want to do. However, as a service provider you don't focus on what you do, you need to focus on solving your customer's problems. That is, you have to do whatever it takes to make your customer successful. That means that you might sometimes perform some tasks that are outside of what you would like to do. There are several different of examples of this.

When high-end consulting companies first get into systems integration, they are surprised that they may have to resell equipment or telecommunication lines at a much lower margin than they are used to accepting. They will ask me, "Why do we have to do that? It will lower our overall margins and make our financials look worse to our investors." The answer is that you have to do that because the customer needs and expects you to do that.

Sometimes the customer doesn't even want to do that work, but it has to because its customers or bosses want it to and it in turn expects its solutions provider to help it. In the late 1990s, Congress passed a law saying that anyone who "fought" in the Cold War was entitled to a "Thank You" certificate signed by the Secretary of Defense acknowledging his or her service. This included all military and government civilian workers who worked for the government from the end of World War II until the Berlin Wall came down. A person wanting this certificate would send documentation to the Army's Software Development Center – Washington (SDC-W). SDC-W would verify the credentials and then print out and mail the certificate. The bulk of the work was running a mailroom, a large room that received mail from all over the country. Clerks would go through the mail, print out certificates, and put them in mail folders for delivery to the post office. It was definitely not the high-tech work that either SDC-W or SRA wanted to be known for. Nevertheless, we gladly accepted this responsibility.

The reason this rule was controversial was that SRA's CEO, Ernst Volgeneau, would accuse me of wanting to run motor pools. He did not want SRA to get into the business of blue-collar services and he thought that this rule would lead to that blue-collar work. I told him that that wasn't necessarily true, but I didn't let on just how close we came. We won a large ($20M/year) job for the Naval Sea Systems Command. Most of the job was high-end information technology, but a portion of the work required us to operate a warehouse with spare parts for the Navy. The labor categories we needed to staff included forklift operators. I never mentioned this part of the project to senior SRA managers. We just used a subcontractor to perform this portion of the work and kept it under the radar. Frankly, I never saw any reason why we shouldn't run a motor pool, especially if that was part of developing and operating an entire logistics system. CEOs do get to set the limits of what they will do, but you need to set these more broadly than most people first think.

Because you do get to choose your customers, but not what you do for them, it is important to choose your customers wisely.

6. The path to growth isn't through your deliverables

Of course it is important to do everything in your statement of work and do it well. But that is not sufficient to make your customer a success or help you grow your work with that customer. Don't be like the pharmacist in Rule 4. A common complaint from government CIOs is that their contractors do only what they are asked to do. They want their contractors to give them advice on what they *should* be doing. Sometimes a Project Manager will tell me that he or she is doing a good job because they do everything their customer asks them to do. When I hear that, it is time to send that PM to a re-education camp.

Many companies perform some sort of customer satisfaction survey. Companies want to use the results of these surveys to figure out if the customer is sufficiently satisfied with their work for them to be awarded the follow-on contract. Of course, you can't ask that question directly. I've found that one of the questions that correlate highly with recompete win rate is the following: "Are we providing innovative solutions?" The fact that we even ask this question on a regular basis is surprising, because most of our contracts do not ask for innovative solutions. Many contracts are Time and Material (T&M) contracts where we are working as staff augmentation, taking our direction, to a large extent, from the government. This question is really a surrogate for questions such as: "Are we making suggestions on how to do our job better?" "Are we suggesting what we should be doing?" "Are we looking for ways to save you money?"

Figure out what you should be doing and suggest that to your customer. And regularly check to see if your customer perceives you as offering more than what they ask.

7. You are not a technology company

Many people in a services company have the made the mistake of thinking they are a technology company. Many of our customers in CIO offices have also mistakenly thought this. We are not a technology company in the sense that Apple, Microsoft or CISCO are technology companies. They are in the business of creating new technologies. We are in the business of applying technology to solve customers' problems. That is a big difference that I hope will become clear throughout this book. The emphasis for a services business needs to be on the customer and its issues, not on technology.

You cannot push technology on a customer. You can lead it, but you can't push technology that it isn't comfortable with. Show how you will improve its mission effectiveness or efficiency through the use of technology. Sometimes the answer is to not introduce new technology, or at least not at the present time. You always need to be focused on what is in the customer's best interest and give advice accordingly.

Many folks in a system integration company go the other extreme and think they are completely vendor agnostic. They believe that they aren't tied to any single product or technical company. It is a good goal to be vendor independent, but you can't fully achieve that goal. No company, no matter how large, can be expert in all of the products in any specific area. No individual is truly vendor agnostic. Everyone has some bias, if only from the fact that they were trained in a limited number of products. If you told me who the database expert was on a project at SRA, I could tell you what database the project was using. I've never met a database expert who was an expert in Microsoft SQL Server,

Oracle, and Sybase. More important, I've never met a database person who didn't have a strong preference for one of these systems over the others. The same is true for operating systems, business intelligence software, and ERPs. Furthermore, a company can't commit to provide training in every product. I tried to select two products (sometimes three) in a space such as business intelligence, database management, or network management. We would commit to having trained people available in those two products. In addition, we could maintain a strong relationship with those two vendors for support. I would tell customers that if they used, for example, Oracle or SQL Server, I could guarantee the availability of trained staff, the ability to reach back to other trained folks for supplementary support as needed, and a relationship with the vendor to assist in problem solving. If they wanted to use a different data base management system, Sybase for example, we could support that on the project, but I couldn't assure them of the same level of corporate support.

The availability of corporate support should be part of the criteria in selecting products for a project. Our project for the Army Housing office, HOMES, almost violated this rule. The project team was selecting a tool to use for business intelligence. They did an independent evaluation and selected a tool that scored highest in the features that a developer thought were "cool" for developing the system. However, the tool was not used elsewhere within SRA or within the Army. I urged our team to conduct a competitive demonstration test between that tool and Cognos, a tool that was familiar to both SRA and the Army. The Army provided test data to both vendors and we asked the vendors to develop a demonstration of how the Army Housing office could use their tool for decision support.

The outcome was easy to predict. The first vendor focused their demonstration on how easy it would be for our programmers to develop the system. The Cognos demo showed how the developed system would make decision support easy for the customer to make functional decisions that were crucial for their business. They showed how their product would improve mission efficiency and effectiveness. The choice was now obvious to everyone. In addition, since we had an organization in the company devoted to supporting business intelligence with Cognos, the project was assured of strong corporate support during development.

Keep your focus on your customer's problem and don't become enamored with any single technology or product. Remember that your job is to apply technology to solve their problems.

8. Hire your competitors

You need to hire from your competitors, but not because you want to drain them of their talent (although that's not a bad idea). You need to hire from your competitors because your company needs some people who think differently. Companies with limited new blood, i.e., where talent is primarily developed in house, find it difficult to adapt to new situations. If you are having difficulty moving into a new area, new technology, or new customer set, and you have invested resources into that initiative, it may be that that new area requires a different way of thinking or a different approach from what you have been doing. If everyone in your company has the same background, you may not be able to grasp what it takes to move into a new area. Cognitive diversity helps you solve new problems. Integrating people who were trained elsewhere is one way to increase the cognitive diversity within your company.

This is a problem not just when attempting to do something new. In the rapidly changing environment that we work in, a company needs to be flexible, and falling into a group-think culture hinders flexible thinking.

It isn't easy for your staff to accept mid-level and senior managers from other companies. Folks will naturally think that an outsider cannot possibly be better than themselves. It is natural to see new folks as competitors. People have to understand that if someone else does well—that is, they help the company grow—something negative has not happened to them. Rather, anything, or anyone, that contributes to a company's growth will ultimately be good for them.

Hiring people from outside of your company is a necessary part of avoiding a group-think approach to problem solving, but it is not sufficient. All of your staff, but especially your middle managers, need to be open to the new ideas that someone from another company will bring. For this to occur, your culture has to have the fundamental characteristic that the best idea wins, regardless of where it comes from. Rule 9 expands on this.

9. Adopt a "best idea wins" culture

Every company will claim that in that company the best idea wins. Don't believe it. This is harder to implement than it appears. This requires a lot more than saying that managers listen to everyone, or rank doesn't matter. The key characteristics that reveal whether this is really the culture are not common in our industry. The best idea cannot win unless folks are trained to draw out the best ideas. That is, the culture must be one of asking questions, not telling. If you don't hear a lot of folks asking questions of others, then you need to rethink your culture in this aspect.

Another key requirement for the best idea to win is for rank or seniority in the company to not matter—at all—when it comes to any discussion. People have to evaluate the idea, not be biased by who is saying it. That is really difficult. I recall one meeting in which a retired military person was acting in a deferential manner toward Ted Legasey, our COO. As we walked out of the meeting, Ted commented to me, "He is not going to advance here." There was no place for anyone who was deferential to superiors. In the early days of SRA there were very few titles for just this reason. Ernst and Ted understood that titles could create problems. They did not want a situation where someone would say, "I'm a GS12, and I'm not going to work for him on this project. He is only a GS11." SRA had only a few titles that indicated a person's status within the company. We worked hard to teach employees that they might be the Project Manager on one project and an individual contributor working on another project. Your position in the company had nothing to do with your role on a project. Project teams were to be constituted based on who the right staff was for that project. We frequently had senior staff working for a more junior project manager. The more a culture has this as an ingredient, the more frequently the best idea will win.

A good example of how this worked at SRA was evident at a senior manager planning meeting. We had recently hired Tony Valletta into the company. Tony was most recently the Acting Assistant Secretary of Defense for Command, Control, Communications, and Intelligence. He was formerly the Vice Director of the Army's Information Systems for Command, Control, Communications, and Computers (DISC4), and he was the senior acquisition official for Army standard management information systems (PEO STAMIS.) He was one of the most respected senior information technology officials in the government. I remember that when Tony was speaking, folks kept interrupting him and contradicting him. While Tony didn't say anything, I could tell that he was not used to such treatment and didn't like it. Later that day, Ernst Volgeneau, SRA's founder and CEO, spoke at our lunch. We treated Ernst the same way, interrupting him and contradicting him. Tony saw that that was just part of our culture. It wasn't anything personal, and Tony quickly adapted to that culture.

You should conduct an honest assessment of the culture of your company with respect to this characteristic. The more that you are truly a "best idea wins" company, the more flexible you will be and the better equipped to face new problems.

10. Company culture is a differentiator

What made SRA different from other companies that started at the same time, but never grew to a billion dollars? The answer has more to do with the culture than with any specific capabilities that we had.

Customers frequently tell me that they can't tell the difference between companies. They say that every company claims to have the same capabilities, their websites all look alike, and they all claim to be able to do everything. Companies may look the same from the outside, but they are different. What differentiates most companies is not technical or functional ability, but culture. Culture affects how we execute a project, the types of projects that we are good at, the types of projects that we are not good at, even the type of person who will succeed or not succeed in our company.

Cultures are not right or wrong, but they do affect the success of a company. During their formative years, SRA and SAIC had very different cultures, but both were able to leverage their cultures in a way that promoted their growth. The employees of SAIC were very proud of the fact that their company was employee-owned. That was an important part of who they were, how they acted, and how they presented the company to their customers.

Cultural differences are obvious to employees, and they are also obvious to customers, but usually not through proposals. Part of the marketing process should be to educate potential customers on the differences. Proposals need to reinforce these differences and make them real. Sometimes it will be in how you manage requirements, develop software, or perform testing.

Sometimes it will be in how you recruit, train, and retain employees. Sometimes it will be in how you interact with your customers. I'll present an example of two different fundamental cultures that describe many of the systems integrators. These cultures can be characterized as either an Engineering Culture or a Customer-based Culture.

The engineering culture is common in those companies whose foundation was building things, such as rockets, airplanes, or ships. Companies whose foundation was primarily analysis have a different approach to executing projects. You will see why I call these cultures "Customer-based Cultures." We can see this difference by examining the two different approaches to quality. The first definition of quality is "conformance to specifications." This approach is described in books such as *Quality is Free*, by Phillip Crosby. Crosby was the quality control manager on the Pershing Missile project. Many companies teach this definition of quality. Some companies even use Crosby's book as a guide. This approach to quality works well with engineering-oriented projects. On this type of project, requirements are defined in detail first and then given to the engineers to build to the requirements. If the engineers build what is specified in the requirements document, they have done a quality job. Note that this definition of quality doesn't evaluate how good the product is, how well it solves a customer's problem, or even whether it works. It only evaluates how well the product conforms to the requirements specification.

The second definition of quality is "Quality is customer satisfaction." W. Edwards Deming was a well-known proponent of this definition. For many information technology projects, the users don't know what they want until they see it. Detailed specifications cannot be fully developed first. Development processes have to be agile, flexible, adaptable, and designed for change. Rather than evaluating the finished product only by how well it conforms to the specifications, it is also evaluated by how well it solves the customer's problem.

One manifestation of this difference is how the company uses functional expertise during development. The engineering companies will use functional expertise primarily to help write the requirements specifications. Companies that have the second approach to quality will integrate functional expertise in all aspects of development, serving as a surrogate user. I'll describe how this works, or doesn't work.

I spent some time as a subcontractor to a major engineering company working on the modernization of the Army World Wide Military Command and Control Information System (AWIS). This company treated us well and even let me participate in much of its training. It was very process-oriented, and trained people in the Crosby approach to quality. However, AWIS was an information system where the requirements could not be specified to the detail that the engineering company was used to on a hardware engineering projects. They failed to deliver software that the user found useful.

In order for AWIS to succeed, the developer needed to engage real users, or at least surrogate users, throughout the life cycle to ensure that the systems that we were building would be useful to a user. These users or surrogate users have a role to play in every phase of development. For example, during testing, it is not sufficient to test only against the requirements documents. Test cases need to be developed based on real-world user scenarios that may go beyond the level of detail in requirements specification. Some folks will say that any test that goes beyond what is detailed in the requirements specification should generate an Engineering Change Proposal (ECP) and perhaps introduce additional cost or schedule to the program. That may be the case, but it is still important to learn about those as early as possible instead of waiting for the user acceptance test. It is best to learn about these during development.

When SRA was the prime contractor for the joint version of the same system, we instituted a user review panel during development which resulted in a successful outcome. A small group of senior influential users from the user community met with us every six weeks or so to review our screens. We would gather their feedback and do a preliminary estimate of any cost or schedule impacts. We would then hold an immediate configuration control board with these power users to decide which changes we needed to put in the next release and which could wait. In this way, we delivered a software product that we knew the users would accept. This approach was successful. This process does require a strong customer who would make sure that only changes that were both necessary and reasonable would be made during development of a release.

This example demonstrates how a company culture affects the way a company performs on a technical project. Company culture affects all aspects of a company's ability to perform. Other aspects of corporate cultures and some ways to strengthen yours are described below.

Aim for engaged employees. Why do very different cultures, such as the cultures at SRA and SAIC, both contribute to growth? The answer is that in both cultures, all employees were committed to the culture. Employees believed in the company and what they could do for their clients. **Employees also believed that they and their company were different from other companies.** SAIC employees were proud that they were an employee-owned company. They believed that that made a difference in how they served customers. SRA's culture involved including functional and technical expertise in everything we did, whether the contract called for it or not. SRA and SAIC both maintained high states of employee engagement. This is something that is measurable. The company, HumanR, conducts a regular engagement survey with participation from many companies in our industry. This tool becomes a mechanism for measuring your own progress and for benchmarking yourself against others in the industry.

Establish a vision that fosters employee engagement. Shortly after I joined SRA, the firm celebrated its fifth anniversary. At the celebration, I recall saying to Ernst Volgeneau, the founder and CEO: "Ernst, you have a great company." His reply said everything: "It's your company too." Ernst had the vision from the early start of the company to create a public company. One runs a public company a lot differently from a private, family-owned company. Even though the company was only five years old at that celebration, I felt that I was part of a long-lived enterprise. We weren't just hired hands working for a single person. The differences became very clear to me.

Years later, after I left SRA, the company that I was running acquired a former small business that was run like the family-owned business that it was. I discovered that the person who served as the executive assistant was charging personal items to the corporate credit card. In most companies this would be grounds for termination. When I confronted her about this, she said that everyone changed personal items to the company credit card. The finance organization kept track of what they owed, and when they could, they paid the company back. Of course our investors could not tolerate that, so I stopped that behavior.

You may think that practices such as this would help create engaged employees, but they can have a very different effect. When companies are managed as a family-owned business, employees become very conscious that they are hired hands working for a single person who holds all the authority. Sometimes the person could be very generous, but he or she could also be capricious and self-serving in how he or she treats employees. I know of one such company where the owner has asked some employees to paint his house. That may help make some employees loyal, but more often the employees in such companies are not fully engaged or committed to the success of the enterprise.

An organization needs to strive to have the staff be loyal to the company, not to their supervisor or other individuals. Too often, when owners run a company as a private venture, their actions are open to complaints of favoritism and similar criticisms.

This drives a culture of mediocrity, rather than one of excellence. Top performers are rarely attracted to such companies.

Tell stories to institutionalize your culture. A company spreads its culture through the telling of stories. At SRA off-sites and at some training sessions, one of SRA's leaders, Barry Landew, would conduct "quizzes" about SRA's history and the company leaders. Questions about our history might include, "Did SRA ever deliver a proposal late?" and he would then describe the history behind it and the lessons learned. "Where was SRA's first office?" was a popular question, especially with new leaders. (Answer: Ernst Volgenau's basement.) Barry would also collect "factoids" from each person at an offsite and at the breaks between sessions have a multiple choice "quiz" to see if folks could guess whose factoid he just read. For example, he would read the factoid "Taught Afro-American history" and suggest three names to choose from. Unless they already knew, no one would guess that it was me. It was a great way to learn something new about our colleagues.

Create a uniform culture. This advice is mostly for those companies that were built mainly through acquisitions. Each division will likely have its own culture. I've seen companies that grow through acquisitions maintain the separate cultures of the acquired companies way too long. There are ways to synthesize those cultures into a single, uniform culture, but it takes deliberate work. Many of the techniques that you will need to apply are the same techniques that most large companies will also need, but it is especially important for companies that have grown mainly through acquisitions. These techniques include:

> **Hold off-sites that mix groups.** And, of course, tell stories at those off-sites. One very large engineering company ensures that the senior staff from new acquisitions participate in all corporate off-sites and, at these off-sites, the new employees are intentionally separated during all activities to ensure that they mix with established employees rather than just stay together. Don't let them stay together

at dinners or social events, either. Even at informal networking events, watch to make sure that the new employees are introduced around the company and are not staying by themselves.

Have a standard new-employee orientation. I see too many companies, especially large companies, where different divisions have slightly different orientations. If you want to create a single culture, start with the new-employee orientation. Don't leave that up to separate divisions. The way to use the new-employee orientation to promote your culture is to have a discussion of your values as the first item in the orientation. This should start with a discussion of the company overall, your values, and what is expected of all employees. I see too many new-employee orientations that start with benefits or some other presentation by the human resources staff. Some companies do a little better and start by presenting a version of their corporate capability presentation that they give to customers. It is much more effective to develop a tailored presentation on the type of company that you want to have, and to have that presented by a senior member of the staff or the company or division president, not a human resources person. There are more suggestions about a company's values in the next rule.

Move people across organizations. This is such a useful technique when trying to create a single culture, that I made it a separate rule, Rule 50.

Your culture will differentiate you from your competitors, so it is important to spend the resources defining and spreading your chosen culture.

11. Your culture is tied to your values

This may seem obvious, but I've met a lot of folks who think that cultures evolve and change over time. If you don't think that the corporate values should change over time, why would you think that cultures should change over time? I'll explain what parts of culture can change and what parts do not, or rather, should not, change over time.

As a company grows, the size and characteristics of the projects that it performs will likely change. Consider a company that evolves into multiple business units. One unit may consist of small, analysis projects staffed by a small number of people with advanced degrees. Another business unit may consist of large projects with 100 people doing lesser skilled work. There will be natural differences between those projects. They will each have their own subculture. But the important cultural aspects of the company do not need to change. If, for example, a core corporate value is "best idea wins," then all of the projects across both units should adhere to that cultural characteristic. Jacobs Engineering provides a great example of how a culture can be strong and still extend across a large $11B global company. Its work encompasses both highly skilled and blue-collar workers. It has work across the globe, so its staff has natural cultural differences. Safety is a core Jacobs value. All of its employees demonstrate an unwavering commitment to safety as a core value and as an integral part of their culture. This is true across all of the projects, and Jacobs puts a lot of effort into instilling that culture in the companies that it acquires. This is just as true on their high-end information technology business units as it is on their construction engineering projects. Their fundamental cultural characteristics do not change across their $11B global projects. There may be noticeable changes in a company as it grows and evolves, but the aspects of the culture that are tied to their values do not change. Those key characteristics of culture will change when, and only when, the company's values change. If corporate leadership holds true to its values, then the company culture will not change.

However, I've seen a lot of examples where company values and culture do change, and they can change easily. Cultures are very fragile. Managers have to Walk the Talk, all the time. Employees will see right through pronouncements that aren't genuine. If the leadership in a company changes and the new leader does not adhere to the values, the culture of a company will change overnight. As described earlier, SRA had a strong culture that supported anyone challenging a leader at any level. The messages from Ernst Volgeneau and Ted Legasey in this regard were very strong. Ted mentioned to me once that if someone was too deferential to authority, he would not advance very high in the organization. However, the culture of SRA did change almost overnight. A new CEO was brought in from the outside, and that new CEO tried to remake SRA into the image of another company. The employees immediately picked up on the change from the top, and the culture changed throughout the organization. Folks were no longer comfortable challenging senior managers and telling them when they disagreed with them. The board of directors and investors recognized that this cultural change had a negative impact on SRA's success and took steps to rectify it. Recapturing lost trust is very difficult and may be impossible. If you want your values to endure, then you can't tolerate a manager at any level who isn't 100 percent committed to your values.

12. Change the rules

If you are competing against much larger companies, you cannot compete on their terms. Of course you can't change the laws dealing with government contracting, but that doesn't mean that you have to play their game on their court. If you do, you'll lose. So what's the alternative? What can you do? The example above in Rule 4 about how we won USAID is one way. That procurement was for providing operations and maintenance services. I'd bet that all of the competitors proposed an approach that attempted to show why their approach to operating a network was better than everyone else's. Frankly, I'd bet that there wasn't much difference among those proposals. Our proposal showed that we could provide those services too. After all, we had to be compliant, and we had to show that our approach didn't have any weaknesses. We took a bold approach and said that providing those services wasn't a big deal. After all, even we could do THAT. But we showed them what else we could do for them. Notice that I said "COULD" do for them. We didn't increase our price by saying that we would do those other things. We just showed them how we would do those things if we were asked.

You have to be bold. Even large businesses have to take a different approach to getting the job done. If it is a cost-plus-award-fee or cost-plus-incentive-fee type of contract, take a different approach to the fee structure. When Unisys first won a big contract for the Transportation Security Agency (TSA) shortly after the attacks of 9/11, it bid an award fee that depended on how many people fly. A major concern of the government was getting the public comfortable with flying again, so proposing that their fee was dependent on how many people fly, the outcome that the government wanted, was a bold, different, and winning approach.

Computer Sciences Corporation (CSC) won a major job for the Defense Commissary Agency by taking an approach that was much different from everyone else's. The agency wanted a commercial-off-the-shelf (COTS) software system for managing their commissaries. Commissaries are supermarkets. The project was to provide a modernized system for operating all aspects of that business. It included a store inventory system, a warehouse system, a financial system, a truck delivery system, and a time-keeping system. There were five bidders. Four of them bid a suite of commercial products that were in wide use within the super-market industry. CSC bid the software that Shaw's grocery stores in the Boston area used to manage their stores. That was a Cobol-based system that Shaw's wrote itself. It was not in use by any other supermarket. While the software that we bid was in use all over the country by major supermarkets, it had the disadvantage of requiring the government to pay annual software maintenance fees, as all commercial software requires. Shaw's software had no license fees. It wasn't maintaining it. CSC's bid was almost $50M lower than our bid. It did not play on the same field as the other four bidders.

13. Do the unexpected

Companies frequently ask me how they can make themselves stand out from their competitors. It seems that everyone can claim to have the same technical expertise, and government procurement rules sometimes force all proposals to look alike in many ways. I tell them that sometimes even the smallest gesture can make you stand out if it is unexpected.

During some procurements, a company will have an opportunity to discuss its proposals in an oral presentation. These are very formal occasions. Before the days of ubiquitous cell phones, I surprised the evaluators (and our marketing people) at an oral presentation for a major opportunity. During the introductions period, as the government evaluators entered the room, it was standard procedure for me, when I was the Program Manager or the senior person from our company, to introduce myself to each person in the room and hand him my business card. On this occasion I wrote my home phone number on the card as a means of expressing my commitment to the program. In the days before cell phones, folks were not available 24/7 and no one had ever given the government people his home phone number. This created quite a stir among the government evaluators. It was a small gesture that made a huge impression.

Another way to do the unexpected is to bid someone who the government perceives is more senior than they expect for that job. When SRA first bid on a large support contract for the Federal Deposit Insurance Corporation (FDIC), it bid Kathy Adams as the program manager. Kathy was a former senior executive at the Social Security Administration and enjoyed an excellent reputation throughout the government CIO community. During the question-and-answer part of the oral presentation, the government asked, "Are we really going to get Kathy Adams?" We knew then that we had won that job.

In times when low cost is more important than best value, it is even more important to figure out how to make your bid different from the pack. If you are bidding a cost-plus-award-fee contract, consider bidding a base fee of zero. Even more important is to be creative in bidding the criteria for your award or incentive fee. Be bold. Offer something that the other companies won't think of. Do the unexpected.

14. Adapt to paradigm shifts

Service companies get into serious difficulty when they fail to quickly adapt to paradigm shifts. If your customers are changing faster than your company is changing, you will quickly lose ground to your competition. The most common paradigm shift has been a technology shift, but there are other major changes that are serious enough to be considered paradigm shifts. As I write this, the government services industry is undergoing paradigm shifts in three areas: technology, acquisition, and budget.

A paradigm shift in technology occurred frequently over the last thirty years, but that change is occurring at an even faster rate today. To illustrate the seriousness of these changes, we can look at the history of the support that Electronic Data Systems (EDS) provided to the Army for computer systems. When I started supporting the Army in the 1980s, EDS was one of the largest supporters of Army computer systems. It operated all of the Army's data centers and provided major support to the development of Army computer systems. In the nineties, it had responsibility for almost all the development for the Army Software Development Center in Washington. Some years later, it had much less work for Army computer systems. While EDS was competent in many technology areas, it was best known for operating large data centers. When the technology moved from large mainframe data centers to smaller, distributed client-server architectures, EDS didn't move quickly enough to adapt and replace its data center work.

The industry went through a similar shift with the move from custom development to ERP implementations. Companies that timed that shift properly built a nice ERP business early and were able to sustain that lead in the industry. Timing is crucial.

SRA was late getting into ERP implementation. We did not want to make the mistake of investing too early. We knew that the government was going to spend a lot of money on ERPs, but we didn't know when it would start, what products it would use, or how we could efficiently build that capability. We waited until ERPs were established in our customer set. This was too late to build this capability from scratch, so we bought a company with those skills. SRA did eventually develop a respectable ERP capability, but the companies that timed the movement to ERPs built a sustainable business model sooner and were able to maintain a competitive lead and capture a larger portion of the market.

Becoming an expert in new technologies does require an investment. You have to send people to training. In addition to the cost of training, you are probably going to have to take them off of direct billable work, so it is frequently a double hit. If you don't immediately have work using those newly learned skills, then you may even have those folks on the bench waiting for work. The worst case is that the people that you train go off to other projects and when you finally do receive work using those skills, you have to train an entirely new set of staff.

When the use of Customer Relationship Management (CRM) software became popular, we knew that the product from Siebel CRM Systems, Inc. was going to gain a foothold in the government. However that took longer than anyone realized. American Management Systems (AMS) made an early investment in training staff in that software, and it eventually did develop a system for the Navy based on Siebel software. However, those projects materialized much later than expected, and I don't think AMS ever recouped its investment.

Currently we are moving to a new paradigm based on cloud computing services. While the government has not moved fully to the cloud, most agencies have initiatives in place to at least explore this change. This is a major shift for companies that provide services. A significant amount of work comes from operating and maintaining the network of a government agency. These networks usually operate on government-owned equipment and operate in government office space. The movement to the Internet cloud will move these operations to a contractor-owned facility running on contractor-owned equipment. The companies that will do best in this new environment will be those companies that define a role for themselves and then invest in building the infrastructure to support that role. They could become a cloud provider, providing the facility and infrastructure to run the government's networks. Or they could adapt to a new paradigm for system development where systems are developed to run on cloud platforms. However you define your value proposition in a cloud environment, it will require that you invest in new skills and establish a marketing and execution approach to fit your new role.

There is also a major change taking place, with the government increasing its use of Low Price/Technically Acceptable (LPTA) acquisitions. This is when the government selects the contractor that proposes the lowest price while meeting the minimally acceptable requirements. This is in contrast to a best-value procurement where the government may agree to a higher price in return for a product or service that provides a better value to the government. Most people assume that the push to LPTA is being driven by the reduced government budgets. I'm sure that budget pressure has something to do with this movement, but when I ask senior government officials why they are using LPTA more, I get a different answer. The consistent answer that I get is, "We can't tell you apart. You all claim to have the same skills; your websites all look alike. Price is the only way we can tell you apart." I asked a senior official at a defense agency why it was using LPTA for a procurement for high-end analytical advisory services. He said, "We have a stable of companies that we know can do this job. Frankly, we don't care if it is you or one of the other companies." I asked how he was going to prevent a lesser-skilled company from "buying" the contract and not being able to perform satisfactorily. He agreed that the RFP needed to clearly set a high bar for "Technically Acceptable." That is one of the few approaches that a company can take to mitigate the effects of LPTA. Work with your customer early to set a high standard for what passes as technically acceptable.

Whether the government was relying more on LPTA or not, the realities of the current environment are that budgets are putting pressure on everyone to achieve more with less money. Companies have to respond with cheaper and smarter proposals. Now more than ever, agencies need contractors that help them make decisions about how they should spend their money. It is no longer sufficient to have the best technical approach. You have to show the government how you will help them through difficult budget times.

Paradigm shifts are creating new problems for incumbents. Incumbent contractors are losing their recompetes at a greater rate than ever before. I have seen some reports that win rates for recompetes are now the same as for new competitions (around 30 percent.) Incumbents are at a disadvantage on both price and technical approach.

There are several reasons why they are at a disadvantage with their price. The first is that the incumbent staff is usually paid more than a new staff likely would cost. The staff has been getting increases over the last five years (or even 10 years), but they are mostly doing the same job they were doing when the contract started five years ago. Someone who is a database administrator, for example, is doing the same job he was doing five years ago, but at a higher salary. You could probably replace that person with a lower paid individual who meets the stated job requirements. If you bid the current rates, it is almost certain that another bidder will underbid you significantly. Facing the choice of lowering your people's salaries or losing is not a good choice. You have to start to deal with this situation a year of more ahead of your recompete. You have to manage the staff on your project so you have planned turnover from the beginning, and you need to structure your bid to assume more turnover over the next contract period too.

Your rates are also higher because when you bid the job five years ago, there was probably less competition. Your overhead rate and perhaps your profit expectations were higher too. While companies are willing to bid lower profit and make internal changes to reduce overhead rates, how do you explain to the customer that suddenly you can charge less? Again, you have to start the process of lowering your costs well ahead of the procurement.

Incumbents are also at a disadvantage because of the rapidly changing technology. Customers don't just want more of the same. They want to see how you are going to help them change with the times. You need to start introducing innovations a year before the recompete acquisition. If the customer sees you as more of the same, and at a higher cost too, you don't stand a chance. Changing your team, adding a specialty subcontractor in a new skill, for example, may help with your image. If you do bring on a new subcontractor, it is always better to bring it onto your team for the current contract and not wait until the proposal to introduce it.

Many companies don't approach a recompete with the same amount of planning that they do for new competitions. I see companies assign their best capture and proposal people to new opportunities while they assume that a business unit can run its own capture for a major recompete with minimal corporate support. This is a real mistake. Capture plans for recompetes need to be developed early and supported in the same way as capture plans for new competitions. One step that is frequently omitted for a recompete is conducting a Black Hat review. In a Black Hat review, you get knowledgeable folks to assume the role of your likely competitors. They develop and present their strategy to beating you. You can then develop approaches to respond to these opposing strategies. For new opportunities, a Black Hat review could give you a competitive advantage. For recompetes, it is a way to reveal your vulnerabilities when you still have time to develop a plan to remove them. It is as important to conduct this review for a recompete as it is for a new competition. I suggest conducting such a review a year (or more) ahead of your recompete so you have time to implement your approach.

Paradigm shifts are the major reason that service companies fail. If you recognize these early and take the appropriate steps to change, you will gain a significant competitive advantage. If you don't change quickly enough, you will put your company in jeopardy.

PART TWO
BUSINESS
DEVELOPMENT

15. You can't sell from behind your desk

Too many people with responsibility for business development or growth spend most of their time in their offices or with business development people from other companies. That doesn't help win new business. My wife, Suzan Zimmerman, Senior Vice President for Strategic Capture at CACI, emphasizes that you can't sell from behind your desk. This is a relationship business, and you can't build relationships unless you spend a lot of time with your future customers. I learned this lesson a long time ago by observing Electronic Data Systems (EDS).

In the early 1990s, The Army Information System Software Center (ISSC) had two companies under an ID/IQ contract called Umbrella 2. The companies were EDS and Lockheed Martin. In those days, the government didn't have to formally compete task orders between the two prime contractors. It could assign a task order to the company that it felt could best perform the task. EDS was awarded all of the work for the Software Development Center-Washington (SDC-W), one of the commands under the Army's Information Systems Software Center. The Commander of ISSC relayed to me that in every quarter, executives from Lockheed Martin would fly to Washington from Owego, New York, complaining that they weren't getting any work. This was the extent of their trying to build relationships with this customer. It was clear to me how EDS was getting all of the work. Every time I went into the office of a manager at SDC-W, there was an EDS person hanging around. EDS understood that the only way to build relationships with customers was to spend time with them. I watched how EDS did this, and I knew that I could do it too.

We decided to bid the recompete, called Umbrella 3, as a prime contractor, and the two winners were EDS and SRA. We didn't win every task over the next five years, but we did win a fair share. We were awarded the task to perform Post-Deployment Software Support for the Army's Sustaining Base Information System before the EDS folks even knew that that task was going to SDC-W. We didn't win everything, of course. The EDS employees certainly knew how to market, and they taught me a lot about staying close to your customer. As I began to market other customers, I took every opportunity to be at the Army's facility. I would plan to have lunch, or morning coffee, in the Army cafeteria as frequently as possible. You never know who you'll meet there. Nothing takes the place of being with your customer. If you can't get breakfast or lunch at your customer's locations, go to the place where people from your industry hang out. In the Northern Virginia area the place to be seen is the Tower Club at Tysons Corner. It is an ideal spot for meeting people. Having breakfast or lunch there is a great way to network with key leaders in the area. I frequently meet industry leaders and customers when I'm there, and I frequently meet with perspective clients in their dining room or the bar after work.

If your business development and sales folks spend most of their time in the office, you need to either re-focus them or get new sales people who understand this rule.

16. People buy from people they like and trust

I've heard the expression, "People buy from people they like" many times. This is another rule that Suzan Zimmerman emphasizes. This is certainly true, but there needs to be more to the relationship than just being someone that the customer likes. You have to be genuinely interested in the customer's success. Zig Ziglar puts it this way: "People don't care what you know until they know that you care." They have to trust that you will act in their best interest and that you can solve their problems and support them. It isn't easy to earn that trust. Most managers don't realize how little their customers trust them. You have to work diligently to overcome that feeling of distrust.

Most government folks think that the only thing that motivates us is higher and higher profit. To compound that problem, government managers usually have a gross misconception of what our profit is. I used to regularly address classes at the National Defense University's (NDU) Information Resource Management College as a representative of the Information Technology of America Association (now TechAmerica). I would frequently ask them what they thought the average after-tax net profit was for a government services contractor. I would frequently get answers such as 20 percent, 25 percent, or even more. On a cost-reimbursable contract, the usual fee was around 8 percent gross. Out of this profit, we had to subtract expenses that were "unallowable" such as entertainment expenses, and we had to pay taxes too. On some items, such as travel, we might not get any fee. Therefore it was impossible to realize double-digit after-tax profits. Fixed price and time and material-type contracts could result in higher profit, but the government regulations are such that the profit for services can't be significantly higher, certainly not 20 percent or 25 percent. This was a difficult concept for most government program managers and even contracting officers to understand. TechAmerica added to its presentation at NDU a section that tried to explain a contractor's cost structure. I was amazed how little the students understood about our real costs.

Since government officials don't understand our costs and have a natural disposition to think that we are motivated only by higher and higher profits, they possess a natural skepticism of our motives. We need, therefore, to work even harder to earn their trust. At SRA, we put a huge emphasis on trust by constantly talking about how we need to always act in the customer's best interest, even when it wasn't in our own best interest. We told stories about times when employees would come to me and ask, "The customer asked us if we should do A or B, but we don't think he should do either. What should we tell him?" Of course the answer is "He shouldn't do either."

A situation where our response surprised everyone occurred when we won the RCAS contract. The government gave us a list of software and hardware products and asked us to renew the maintenance agreements with the vendors. This was a fixed-price contract and the total amount of yearly agreements was around $4M. As we worked to renew these agreements, we learned that many of them had already been renewed. We informed the government that we would be returning a large amount of money that we didn't need. The government contracting person said that we didn't need to do that. This was a fixed-price contract and we were entitled to the full amount. Furthermore, if we learned that there were even more products that we had to renew, they would not have given us more money, but they would have held us to our fixed-price proposal, so they felt it was fair for us to keep the full amount. Nevertheless, we insisted that we return some of the money. This was the start of a longtime relationship.

Gaining the trust of the customer and making him believe that you are the best company to solve his problems frequently requires a team of folks. In order to close a deal, you have to have three roles covered with people that the customer likes and trusts: a Project Manager, a Technical Lead, and a Sales Person. The Project Manager is the single point of contact responsible for the project's success. The technical lead is someone the customer trusts to solve his technical problems and produce the deliverables. The sales person is the person responsible for ensuring that customer meetings are set up, the proper follow-up occurs for any meetings, and any requested white papers or documentation are delivered to the customer on time. This doesn't have to be three different people, but these are three distinct roles that one, two, or three people have to play.

It is not sufficient to be liked by a customer. I know a lot of former government and military personnel who are very friendly with current government executives but can't sell any business. It takes a lot more than just being friendly. The customer has to trust that you and your company are the best choice for solving his problems.

17. Play man-on-man, not zone

To use an analogy from basketball, there are two ways to play defense: man-on-man coverage and zone coverage. In the service business, you play both offense and defense, using man-on-man coverage. For each key individual in the customer set, you should have one, and only one, person identified as the lead from your company who covers that individual. Each lead has the responsibility for building a relationship with their assigned individual, knowing everything that is useful about the client, and making sure that the other people in your company have the knowledge necessary to successfully bid and execute work for that individual. Once you build those relationships, it is important to maintain them. At one major company, once a senior person established a relationship with an individual client, he maintained responsibility for that relationship even if there was a reorganization where the work no longer reported to him. That is how important the individual relationship is.

This man-on-man approach differs from a zone approach. In a zone approach, customer relationships are established not by customer or organization but by either functional or technical responsibility. Many companies are organized this way, and they are playing zone, sometimes without giving it much thought. This inevitably leads to territorial disputes within an organization and inefficient marketing. One of the complaints that I hear most frequently from Program Executive Officers (PEOs) in the Department of Defense is that several people from a company would be simultaneously marketing the PEO and not knowing what the others in their company were doing. This happens frequently with PEOs, since their charters may be so broad that several different business units all believe that they are marketing in their assigned area. For example, the Army PEO for Enterprise Information Systems (EIS) is responsible for building systems in several domains. Among them are: finance, human resources, logistics, medical, and base-level support systems. In addition, he is responsible for modernizing communications at Army bases. A company may think it has a reasonable organization structure with, say, its health business in a separate business unit. But what happens when the PEO EIS is tasked with building a health-related system? All too often, the business units don't even coordinate their marketing efforts and meetings. PEOs don't like that. The company doesn't look good either. Someone needs to be tagged with playing one-on-one with the PEO and has to coordinate and be a part of all meetings and marketing efforts with that office.

18. Assign an account manager

We discussed in the first section the importance of understanding and solving your customer's underlying problem. This is one of the keys to growing out a customer. For example, you are awarded a task for information assurance or software development, or maybe help desk. You are doing a great job for that customer, and you want to expand your work by selling more of your capabilities to that customer. It may be necessary to establish a relationship with someone above your immediate government program manager or contracting officer with whom you can discuss their broader problems. You have to play everyone in the customer's organization man-on-man as I described in the previous rule. Someone has to be responsible for identifying the decision makers and building a relationship with them, one-on-one.

The problem is that your PM on site may not be the right person to do this. There are several possible reasons why your on-site PM may not be selling more of your company to his or her customer. The PM is probably nose-down, fully occupied trying to get his or her deliverables produced. Your PM may be an expert in a special area, such as information assurance, but may not be knowledgeable enough about other areas to pursuade the customer that you can solve a broader problem. In order to identify and discuss a solution to an underlying problem, you may need to work with someone other than the immediate customer PM or COTR. Your PM may not have the time to build a relationship with someone above or outside the immediate customer, or your PM may not be senior enough in the eyes of the customer to establish a personal relationship with the decision maker. If not your PM, someone has to be assigned to identifying the decision makers with the broader, underlying problems, identifying those problems, and working with that customer on how to best solve those problems.

At SRA, we had plenty of examples of where we did this well and where we did it poorly. I'll start with an example of where we didn't do this at all and missed opportunities to grow out a customer.

Around 2005, SRA was performing on or had completed at least six jobs for the Internal Revenue Service (IRS.) We were performing well on an information assurance task, we were successful on several software development tasks, and we implemented Tivoli, an enterprise management product, to over 120,000 IRS users. This was the largest Tivoli implementation anywhere to date. At one point we were performing on around $25M/year for the IRS. At that time, I met with a senior person in the IRS CIO office. The IRS had recently awarded a large system development job to a competitor. The IRS official said that when they were discussing who could do this new job, SRA's name didn't even come up. He said that the senior folks at IRS viewed SRA as a niche player. We were performing well on six different tasks, and yet they viewed us as a niche player, not a systems integrator.

Contrast this with what happened with our work for the National Guard Bureau (NGB). We were the Program Management Support Contractor for the Reserve Component Automation System (RCAS.) SAIC was the systems integrator for that project. Our role was that of a typical PM support contractor. For example, we evaluated the SAIC Quality Assurance plan, and we helped prepare briefing slides for the government. It was not a technical job. After a few years of our being the RCAS PM support contractor, two jobs that EDS was performing for the National Guard Bureau were coming up for recompete. These jobs were not directly related to RCAS. One job was operations and maintenance of the Army's wide area data and video conferencing networks, called GuardNet 21. The other job was operations and maintenance of the National Guard Bureau's distance learning network called the Distributed Technology Training Program (DTTP.) The NGB decided to combine these two jobs into one program. One day, Mike Yocom, who was running our Army business unit, came to me and said that the NGB Deputy CIO said to him, "You ought to bid this job." I was certainly surprised. Our work for the NGB wasn't anything like running a network. In fact, SRA didn't even do much in the way of network operations in those days. Did he really think SRA was a viable competitor or was he just trying to drive up the competition? Shortly after this conversation, the Deputy CIO and I got into a conversation at the annual National Guard Association conference. He said to me, "You ought to bid this job." We did bid it, and we won.

Why did the NGB see us as being able to solve broader problems even though we were doing only one job, and a nontechnical one at that, while the IRS saw us a niche player even though we were performing on six different jobs? The answer is that for the NGB, we had someone playing the role of account manager playing man-on-man with the government decision makers. Mike Yocom used the RCAS project to start every Friday morning at the NGB. Since he was a senior person with much broader experience than our RCAS PM, Mike was able to spend time on the top floor of the NGB building and build a relationship with the senior government officials. After a few years, they came to understand that Mike, and SRA, could help them solve their broader, underlying problems better than the usual systems integrator. At the IRS, no one served in that role. Each of our PMs focused on their individual problem. Also, these PMs came from different organizations within SRA. No one (other than the company CEO and COO) had overall responsibility for growing the IRS business. We were playing zone against the IRS, and we missed major opportunities.

19. Zipper up!

This is an extension of playing man-on-man. Government organizations have a hierarchy of positions. Your approach needs to mirror their organization structure. Just like the two sides of a zipper coming together, you need to assign a counterpart to each person in your customer's hierarchy. The government loves the concept of counterparts. Each person in the government likes to know who his counterpart is. Project organizations need to mirror as closely as possible the customer's organization, or at least make it crystal clear who the counterpart is to each of the government's task managers. Many RFPs will ask to see this, usually by asking that proposals show "lines of communication." This applies to every task lead on a project as well as the government managers above the project. It applies to all circumstances. When I first started as a project manager, I didn't see the value of having my contracts person present in every meeting where I discussed a deliverable with my customer. After all, these were technical discussions. But it was quickly pointed out to me that the government had its contracts person present, and she wanted her counterpart present.

The zipper rule also applies to doing business with other companies. In addition to whatever working relationships are established, the senior manager (e.g., Vice President) should establish a relationship with his counterpart from the other company. If you establish a teaming relationship with another company, it is not sufficient for your business development staff to have a relationship with their counterparts. The business unit leaders must also establish a personal relationship. Without a trust relationship that goes up the zipper, it will be difficult to resolve issues when they arise.

Business is done by people. Without personal relationships at all levels, you can't have a positive business relationship with customers, partners, or suppliers.

20. Lead with your right

When you are selling to the government, especially the Department of Defense, you need to demonstrate both technical and mission (functional) understanding. The customer needs to meet and be comfortable with your folks who cover both of these knowledge sets. In order to close a deal, the customer is going to want to know the person who will have ultimate responsibility for the job and the person who will be the technical lead or the person responsible for solving his/her problems.

There are two different types of customers. In the Department of Defense, these two types have different roles by law. The same principles apply to civil government, but the roles are sometimes less clear. I'll describe the two types of customers and how you should approach them differently. I'll use the Department of Defense for the example.

The two types of customers are: 1. Those that have mission responsibility and 2. Those that are fundamentally technical organizations that acquire, build, or supply systems and solutions for the type 1 customers. Examples of the first type are the combatant commands, Air Mobility Command, and the Army Human Resources Command. Examples of the second type are the Program Executive Officers (PEOs) and the Defense Information Systems Agency (DISA.) By law, major acquisitions are the responsibility of the PEOs. In civil government and many commercial organizations, the type 2 customer is the internal CIO organization that provides solutions to the functional organization (finance, services, operations, marketing).

If you are selling to a functional command, your lead should be someone who understands that mission, preferably someone who came out of that organization. That person needs to be supported by the right technical staff to offer a combination of functional and technical expertise. Because of this rule, some folks think that only those who have been in the military can take the lead in selling to the military or building a defense business. That isn't true, because Defense usually acquires services and products through the PEOs, not the functional commands.

If you are selling to a PEO or one of the system commands, you should recognize that those folks are primarily technical, solution-oriented folks. The same person might work throughout his career on different types of systems including personnel systems, command and control systems, HR systems, and medical systems. When approaching those offices, you should lead with the proper technical staff and have them supported with the right set of functional expertise.

You always offer a combination of functional and technical expertise, but you lead with your functional person or your technical person, depending on the type of organization and person you are meeting with. Lead with the right person and you will be off to the right start.

21. Good proposals don't win

When I became President of TechTeam Government Solutions, I held a series of all-hands meetings with our employees. One of the first questions I was asked was, "We write good proposals. Why don't we win more?" The superficial answer is that everyone writes good proposals. It takes an outstanding, compelling proposal to win. But more specifically, what could TechTeam do differently to create a compelling proposal? Most government agencies are very good at identifying the strengths and weaknesses in a proposal and conveying that information in a debriefing to the losing company. In reviewing TechTeam's recent bids and debriefings, I saw that its proposals had very few weaknesses identified. It also had very few strengths identified.

Proposals that win have strengths that can be identified in every section and subsection. This is very different from the approach that many companies take to creating their proposals. The usual approach to starting a proposal is to assemble smart people who understand the customer and have them create a handful of "themes" that are supposed to drive a winning approach and proposal. These themes are supposed to discriminate the proposal from a competitor's proposal and give the government reasons why they should select that company. The final draft of a proposal is reviewed by a Red Team before it is submitted to the government. These reviewers evaluate and score the proposal. One of the items that they look for in their evaluation is checking to see if the themes are obvious to the reader. Unfortunately, on almost every proposal Red Team the comment "The themes aren't visible" is made. A more serious problem that many Red Teams don't even recognize is that frequently there aren't a lot of strengths in most of the sections. The best sections may get a score of "compliant," but few sections receive a score of "outstanding." Most sections in the average Red Team review are scored "yellow," meaning something is missing. That is, the review team does not think that the government evaluator will give that section a winning score. You have to shoot for a score of "outstanding" in every section. Not just an outstanding theme in the executive summary or introduction, but outstanding ideas that an evaluator can call out as a strength in **every** section.

Unfortunately, the proposal process that most companies follow isn't designed to drive out strengths in every section. During the typical proposal process, the small number of high-level themes is passed to the technical staff. At Red Team review, you then discover that the section on, for example, desktop virtualization doesn't reflect any of those themes. Why did you think it would? The average technical writer is not going to be able to translate a high-level theme into a strength for his approach to desktop virtualization. High-level themes are important and do need to be clear, especially in the executive summary. However, the person writing a lower-level section will have no idea of how to apply that theme to the section on testing, or help desk operations, or recruiting.

What is needed is a proposal process that is designed to inject into every section at least one idea that an evaluator can identify as a strength. That is, the proposal writers need to identify some idea in every section that will look to an evaluator as different from and better than what they read in your competitors' proposals. As a consultant to many companies, I hear people say, "There isn't anything special about our solution at the detailed technical level. How do we describe a differentiator?"

Fortunately, there is a way to have your proposal process focus on ensuring that strengths appear in every section. The way to introduce a strength into every section is to use a gatekeeper, as described in the next rule.

22. Use a "gatekeeper" for writing proposals

In the previous rule, I described why most good proposals don't win. Every section of your proposal needs to have something that differentiates your solution from the competition's solution. There needs to be a differentiator, a strength, in every section. This rule describes how to do that.

What is needed is someone—I'll call that person the gatekeeper or thought leader – to ensure that every section contains at least one discriminator that an evaluator can call out as a strength. This is how they work. Before a writer is allowed to start writing full sentences, he needs to explain to the gatekeeper what his key ideas, features and benefits, and discriminators are. Sometimes a brainstorming session with a small group can do this for a small proposal. For larger proposals the gatekeeper works with each writer individually. If the gatekeeper doesn't think that the writer has identified sufficient discriminators or strengths, he will send the writer back to his desk to try again to come up with winning ideas. The gatekeeper and writer might iterate several times before the writer is given permission to start writing prose. If the writer is unable to come up with these on his/her own, the gatekeeper will ask questions to try to draw out of the technical or management approach what is different and better than another approach. This way, each section is reviewed for its key content, strengths, and weaknesses before the Red Team.

Proposal managers are usually not the persons to be this gatekeeper/thought leader. Most proposal managers are too focused on the process, making sure that all work stays on schedule and budget and the proposal is compliant. It takes a senior person focused on the content to drive winning content in every section.

The gatekeeper approach differs from many standard approaches to proposals which have the writer developing features and benefits and diagrams before writing. With the gatekeeper approach, reviews occur as the writer needs them, usually several times a day. In the typical approach, the writer's "story board" is not reviewed until a scheduled review date.

Reviews tied to the calendar are never sufficient. If the only reviews that you hold are those reviews that are held because this is Tuesday and our Red Team is scheduled to review all sections, you will not produce your best proposal. Some sections will be ready for review sooner and some later and some will never contain strengths without one-on-one prodding from someone else. There needs to be a review process that maximizes your calendar time. Go ahead and hold a traditional Red Team, but make sure that you do two things first: have a thought leader work with the writers to drive out features and benefits (strengths and discriminators) before any writing starts, and have someone review the work as soon as it is ready for review without waiting for a specific calendar date.

The gatekeeper approach solves two problems: (1) It helps to drive out winning ideas in every section, and (2) It fixes the inefficiencies of calendar-driven reviews.

23. Be (a little) arrogant

If you don't have high self-esteem or you lack confidence, you won't achieve your potential. You have to be even more than just confident. You need to believe and act as if you are the best. This is true even for large companies, but it is essential that everyone in a small or mid-size company act this way. It was Barry Landew who first taught me this lesson. Barry would proclaim that we were the "best" at something so often that we all came to believe it. People did confuse our strong self-confidence with arrogance, but it was a necessary component in our growth. When we were small and competing against much larger and better-known companies, we had to believe that we were better. We worked hard at being better, too. We didn't just say it. We needed to back up our claims, and there were times when we were able to demonstrate that we were better. We did deliver systems after much larger and more established companies failed. Rule 35 describes how we were able to develop a modernized World Wide Military Command and Control System after a major engineering company failed during the five years that they held the contract. We had to believe that a customer was better off hiring us than a competitor, and the key was to make sure that that was true.

I recall one example where a former Army officer was refusing to market to his friends who were still in uniform. He said to me, "I don't sell to my friends." I replied, "Do you think they will be better served by hiring company X over us?" He answered, "No, we would do a better job." After that he understood that his friends would be better served by the performance and attention that he and SRA would give them. You have to believe in yourself and your company and believe in your heart that your customer's best interests will best be served by you and your company. Believing that you are the best is the first step in becoming the best. Believe it and make it real.

One of the best examples of strong self-confidence bordering on arrogance paying off was what Statistica International was able to accomplish with the modernization of the Army's personnel system, SIDPERS-3. Around 1988, the Army was planning to modernize its personnel system, called SIDPERS-2.75. Statistica was a small company without any technical expertise; it was the functional trainer on SIDPERS-2.75. Dennis Roberts was the business development person at Statistica. Dennis decided to convince the Army to award the development of SIDPERS-3 to Statistica as a set-aside for small disadvantaged business and to award it to Statistica without competition. He believed that the Army would be better served by having Statistica, a tiny company, build the next generation of the Army personnel system than it would be by having an established large business develop the system. It took a lot of nerve to make that case to the Army. Dennis proposed a team where SRA would be responsible for the software development, Martin Marietta would be responsible for test and quality assurance, and Statistica would be responsible for overall project management and training. I thought that it was a worthwhile pursuit. I remember saying to my managers at SRA that I wanted to help Statistica persuade the Army to award it this job as a sole-source set-aside. Everyone at SRA thought I was crazy. "The Army will never trust the modernization of its personnel system to a small disadvantaged company, especially one with no technical expertise," they said. They agreed that I could work on the capture provided that it didn't take too much of my time and I didn't ask for any other resources. Dennis and I proceeded to market the Army. It took us a year, but we did get the contract. Without being bold and projecting extreme self-confidence, we never would have gotten very far with this customer. We worked hard to make it real. We did deliver a new personnel system to the Army. Believe you are the best, and work hard to make it real.

24. Bid as one company

When SRA had revenue of several hundred million, we regularly competed against companies who were very much larger, with revenues in the $3B-$9B range or more. We wondered how we could ever compete against such large companies, whose resources were so much larger than ours. Then we realized that we weren't competing against all of Northrop Grumman, for example. We were competing against one part of one division or maybe one part of one floor of one of their buildings, and we were probably larger than that. So if we could compete as one company, we could compete on almost an equal footing. We put a lot of emphasis on promoting this idea. We emphasized this for two reasons. We had to convince our folks that we really could compete with the large companies on an equal basis. This was a necessary part of getting everyone to be a little arrogant. People needed to really believe that we were at least as good as the big guys. The second reason was that bidding as one company really did give us an advantage. We could bid key personnel from any division in the company, so we were drawing on a relatively large staffing pool. We could easily draw on technology developed anywhere in the company knowing that we could deliver what we promised. When I evaluate companies on their ability to bid as one company, I ask what their process is if one division wants to bid someone from another division as a key person. If the process appears to be cumbersome, then I suggest ways to streamline it. You need to encourage bidding people across divisions, not make it difficult.

If you have a serious commitment to a one-company approach, you will have a competitive advantage in both bidding and executing projects. Go beyond mere words and training programs, and make it real in practice.

25. Marry tactical and strategic marketing

Tactical marketing is targeting specific opportunities to bid. Of course you need to keep a focus on your pipeline and what you are going to bid next. Most companies have a process for tracking and reviewing their pipeline. Some people believe that doing this is sufficient for strategic planning. It's not.

Strategic marketing is targeting customers. It is important that discussions and plans of a strategic nature are also a part of your approach. I believe that you choose your customers. Strategic marketing is choosing your next set of customers, even before there is a near-term procurement that is on your pipeline. I always asked my managers, "Who are your next two customers?" Sometimes this discussion takes place at an annual planning session; sometimes I'll ask this question more frequently. There are several criteria for choosing customers, some obvious, some perhaps not so obvious. Good candidates for future customers are those that:

1. Have money for contractors. This means that they have a budget for contractors, not just a large budget.

2. Have the kind of work you want to do.

3. Have multiple contractors.

4. Use multiple contract vehicles.

5. Are adjacent to current work either as customers or type of work.

The reason that I like to pursue new customers who are already using multiple contractors through multiple contracts is that those are the customers who are easiest to break into with a small task. Obtaining a new, large customer can be done in two fundamental ways. First, you can pursue a large opportunity, put a lot of resources into the capture, and win that work. The second type of pursuit is to target a customer with the above characteristics and work to get a small contract or task order, usually based on some specialty expertise. You then work to build out your share of the customer's budget over time. The amount of money that a customer has for contracting out work is called its "wallet." The Customer Relationship Management (CRM) gurus such as Don Peppers and Martha Rogers taught us that you have to focus on wallet share, not just market share. In the professional services industry that supports the federal government, the market is over $250B. Focusing on market share is not helpful. Focusing on the wallet share of your selected customers is the way to keep a focus on both strategic and tactical marketing.

There are lots of approaches to building out your wallet share of a new customer. One proven approach to eventually winning a large development or operations and maintenance job is to first sell a small decision support or business intelligence system. These systems frequently can be built as add-ons to existing systems and don't require any rework to the existing system. You sell the senior decision makers by providing them with better information, rather than just data, so they have actionable information on which to make decisions. Then sometime later (perhaps even years later), when the customer is ready to start a new effort to modernize the current system, you are in a great position to pursue that modernization effort.

The key to this approach is to pursue a small task that gets a toe in the door and positions you for future work. However, not all small tasks are of equal value in this regard. Not all $300K tasks are the same. Some have potential and are worth a lot more than others. The task should give you some insight into the customer's fundamental business. It should also be a task that shows the customer that you have the knowledge and skills to help it. And the customer must be one whose future budget and contracting dollars makes for a good business case as a future customer. You have to focus on the life-value of a customer, not just the value of the task at hand. If the $300K task is all the customer has, then that task is a dead end. If, however, the customer has a large "wallet" and the $300K task is just a toe in the door, then there is real potential to this customer and worth some effort marketing a small task.

I applied this principle to marketing the National Guard Bureau. The NGB CIO office asked us if we could provide a single analyst to support it. Most folks looked at the opportunity to provide one person in a staff-augmentation role to the CIO office as a dead end not worth much effort. They suggested that we provide a rather junior person with not much of a future for that position. But I didn't do that. I believed that the National Guard was a strategically important customer. We proposed Minter Alexander for that role. Minter was a retired Air Force three-star lieutenant general. He served effectively as the Air Force Comptroller. Minter quickly became a trusted senior advisor to the NGB. That assignment was never expanded. It remained a one-person job. However, it gave our account manager, Mike Yocom, a reason to visit the CIO offices on a weekly basis. This allowed Mike to establish a relationship with key people in that office and to gain an understanding of the fundamental problems that the NGB was trying to solve. This understanding, together with the trust relationships that were built with the staff, eventually led to significant new business.

The other key to strategic marketing is "Don't be fooled by empty revenue." Two examples of empty revenue are: (1) Hardware sales in a service company, and (2) pass-through revenue. The first type is self-explanatory. Here is an example of the second type of empty revenue.

There was a period when the Department of Defense dictated that any new development had to start with a Business Processing Re-engineering task and that that work would use a contract that SRA just happened to have in place, called CIM. Most all of the actual work on that contract was performed by other companies, but SRA was able to recognize all of the revenue, which amounted to over $300M. The profit from that work certainly helped SRA, but the project had little lasting effect on the company. When CIM ended, no follow-on work was identified. No one was hired to support this project. After the project was over, there was no lasting legacy, either in continuing work or in the people hired into the company.

If you compare this project to a seemingly less significant project, the differences become clear. One of our first software development jobs was as a subcontractor to TRW on a project called AWIS (the modernization of the Army's Command and Control System.) We had around 30 people developing software for the Army. That gave us the reputation and technical qualifications to become the lead for the development of the Army's personnel system, which further increased our reputation and technical expertise. We were then able to win, as the prime contractor, the project to develop the modernized command and control system for the Department of Defense. Many of the folks we hired for the initial project went on to become leaders in other projects at SRA. The initial AWIS projects left a future legacy. AWIS led to hiring key people, increasing corporate qualifications, and improved processes.

While it didn't generate as much revenue on any one contract as did the CIM project, AWIS left a lasting legacy in ways that CIM didn't. That is what strategic marketing can do for a company.

If you are getting or relying on empty revenue, go ahead and exploit it and the margins that it provides. You don't have to give it up. Just don't get into the position of needing that entire margin to make your numbers. Focus on how to use that pass-through work to grow the core business. We could have used CIM better. For hardware sales, commit to invest a portion of the "extra" margin in either marketing or talent training.

Tactical and strategic marketing aren't as different in practice as I make them out to be, but the thinking is different. Always ask, "Who are your next two customers?"

26. Use specialties to penetrate new customers

Finding the balance between being a systems integrator and having niche specialties to sell is one of the challenges of our business. Every company spends time trying to figure out the role that new specialties will play in its organization. Some of the questions that have to be addressed are: How much should we spend on developing these skills? How should I organize for supporting and selling these services? How should it affect our branding? For that matter, should it affect our branding? Successful companies figure out how to be known for being both a systems integrator and a company with recognized specialties. That is one of the major characteristics of successful service companies. You need to be expert in something to even get your foot in the door with new customers or, if you are small, with prime contractors. But you can't grow to be a large company if you focus only on a few specialties. I ask many mid-sized companies how they came to be expert in a new technical area. A frequent answer is, "We were doing A for this customer and they asked us if we could do B. We said sure, and figured out how to do that." Specialties are your entrance point into new customers. Once in, the key is to focus on solving the customer's underlying problem, not just the task at hand. That is the other important lesson that successful large companies learned.

Examples of specialties are: Information Assurance, Business Intelligence, Enterprise Systems Management, Business Process Re-engineering, Statistical Analysis, Program Management Support, and Natural Language Processing. Once you select a specialty that you believe you can sell and which will serve as an entry point for your growth, you have to develop a plan (and a budget). Developing a specialty generally requires an approach to people, processes, and tools. People are of course important, because you have to have staff trained in your specialty. Your processes are a significant part of what makes you different from other companies with the same specialty. The tools that you use to accomplish your processes may be tools that you develop, commercial off-the-shelf tools, or a combination. You almost always need some sort of tool.

The first step is to develop *your* process/solution and name that process. Frankly, naming the process sometimes occurs before you define it. Naming something makes it real. When we first set out to define SRA's life cycle development methodology, the first thing we did was to come up with a name. Emerson Thompson was the person who first coined the name ELITE for Enterprise Life Cycle and Technology Engineering. ELITE is still used today as SRA's brand for its solutions. Once you have even a high-level diagram of the process and a name, you can produce a marketing brochure or one-page marketing sheet and try it out on current or potential customers. Just be prepared to have folks trained in the approach when the work starts.

Chris McGoff, in his book *The Primes*, says, "Naming is an essential first step toward achieving mastery over any aspect of life." Chris is the founder of The Clearing, a strategic management consulting firm. He was also a founder of Touchstone Consulting Group, a company that SRA acquired while I was COO.

Create a specialty by giving it a name, define a process that you will use, create marketing material, and train your staff, and you will be on your way to having a specialty offering that drives new business.

27. Invest in GWACs and ID/IQs

Government services are often acquired through the use of umbrella contracts called by various names, such as Government-Wide Acquisition Contracts (GWACs), Indefinite Delivery/Indefinite Quantity (ID/IQ) contracts, or Blanket Purchase Agreements (BPAs.) Commercial companies and state and local governments have similar mechanisms for acquiring products and services in a way that limits competition to a set of pre-qualified vendors.

Many companies win one of these contract vehicles, but are unsuccessful in exploiting them and winning business through them. I would bet that almost every large company in the government services industry has some contract vehicles through which it has never done any business. If you invest wisely in promoting these contracts, they substantially help you grow your business.

Some of these contracts can be used by any government agency. These are called Government-Wide Acquisition Contracts (GWACs). There are only three agencies that have the authority to issue GWACs. They are the General Services Administration (GSA), the National Aeronautics and Space Administration (NASA), and the National Institutes of Health (NIH). Other agencies have their own ID/IQ contracts under many different names.

SRA was the most successful company using the NIH contract CIO-SP (Chief Information Officers-Solution Partners). While SRA did build a successful business at NIH, much of its use of CIO-SP came from other agencies, including the Department of Defense. They did not do this by just sitting back and waiting for RFPs to come to them. SRA, like other companies who were successful with these contracts, built a GWAC organization that helped the rest of the company use their contracts.

There are several different models for funding a GWAC organization, but all of the successful models involved some degree of initial investment. One large company charges a small internal management fee to projects that use its contract. The service that it provides is so useful to the programs that it makes sense for its programs to absorb this charge. While that GWAC center is now self-funding, initially the company had to make an investment to start and promote the center to a point where it would become self-sufficient. At SRA, we funded the GWAC center out of corporate G&A funds, but the principle was the same. We kept track of what business we derived from the center and evaluated its performance accordingly.

At first, the SRA GWAC center had purview over only true government-wide vehicles (GSA schedules, NIH CIO-SP). We found that the center provided such a useful service that when I was Director of the Defense Sector, we asked the GWAC center to take over management of some of our agency-specific ID/IQs. The GWAC center in those days was run by Jeffrey Westerhoff. He worked hard to build relationships with the government contracting officers. He understood how the different contracts worked and what made a winning proposal. He wasn't usually the person who had a relationship with the end-customer who had the requirement and the money, but he was the person who made it easy for the customer to contract with us. When one of our project managers or account managers would identify new work, they would call our GWAC Center. The center would then do most of the work required to get that work under contract. It would work with the customer to identify the best contract to use for its purpose. It would work with the government contracting staff to facilitate the relationship between the contract staff and the end customer, and they would assist in writing the proposal.

The GWAC center staff didn't sell in the traditional sense. They marketed internally to our projects and facilitated the relationship with the government contract office. In that way, they became a valuable resource and key to our growth.

28. The business cannot scale linearly (Business Development)

There are two applications of this rule. One is to business development and the other is to company operations. I'll describe the application to business development here and describe the application to operations in the next section. I've seen a lot of companies with revenue in the range of $50M to $100M. Many of these companies have a lot of small projects, perhaps as many as 100. If your company has $10M in revenue and has, say, 100 projects (much like SRA at one time), you can't grow to $100M in revenue with 1,000 small projects, and at $1B revenue, you certainly can't make it work with a million projects. Just the effort of pursuing that many new proposals would be unmanageable. It isn't reasonable to have a business development and sales staff that pursues that many small jobs.

That means that you have to continually pursue larger projects. These projects probably don't look like your current projects. They will have different characteristics. While this seems like it should be obvious, it isn't obvious to many companies that I support today, and it wasn't obvious to many people at SRA. They thought that we could become a billion-dollar company and still look like we did when our revenues were $100M. Even folks who understand the challenge don't always understand how to make it happen.

There are two categories of issues that arise in pursuing larger and larger projects.

People issues. Folks aren't thinking about larger jobs. People who spent their professional career pursuing jobs in the hundred-thousand-dollar range frequently don't think they can win a job in the hundreds of millions range. People have to first believe that the company can successfully execute a job that is larger than they have ever seen before. This takes some arrogance, but it is necessary.

Marketing changes. You have to realize that growth is going to come from very different types of jobs. When SRA was around $100M in revenue, some folks thought our growth was going to be driven by our special capabilities such as natural language processing, data mining, and information assurance. Those capabilities had never produced revenue greater than a couple of hundred thousand dollars on a project and amounted to a very small percentage of our revenue even at $100M. It wasn't reasonable to think that those offerings would be the engine to drive us to $500M or $1B in revenue. If we pursued only these specialties and the same type of work we currently had, we would have to have a million projects (with commensurate growth in the number of indirect staff for contracts, accounts receivable, and human resources.) Once the senior managers realized this, they were more open to asking what skills we should develop in order for us to become larger. The answer for SRA was to pursue jobs as a systems integrator.

It may be obvious that a large company needs to pursue large opportunities, but it is less obvious that small businesses have to pursue large opportunities too, at least opportunities that are large to them. I worked with a small $20M company that told me that it submitted 45 proposals last year. Most of these were no larger than its current contracts. The chances of significantly growing would increase if it bid four or five jobs worth $10 million or $20 million. Winning one large job would significantly propel the firm's growth.

29. Stretch

The previous rule explains why you always need to pursue larger jobs. The key to real growth is to target opportunities that are game changers. That is, opportunities that are bigger than you have ever won or even bid before. You have to target opportunities that some people in your organization will think you can't possibly win because of your size. The first step in bidding these larger jobs is to think as if you are larger than you really are.

While it is difficult for most folks to think of bidding jobs larger than they have ever seen before, it is even more difficult when a company has grown through acquisitions. I know of billion-dollar companies that think like $30M companies because everyone in the company came from a small acquisition. Everyone has to learn to bid jobs that are larger than the company has ever bid before. While this is crucial for small and mid-sized companies, it applies to large companies too. There are two "tricks" that can help get the message across, especially in smaller companies.

1. **List jobs in the pipeline by $M only, not $K.** This is a trick that Gary Nelson taught me. Gary was a leader of SRA. He was one of the first Vice Presidents and was later appointed Vice Chairman of the Board. Gary led business development for several years and taught us how to focus on larger bids. This was one of his "secrets" that served us well. A $600,000 bid is listed in reports as $0.6, not $600. The psychological effect is greater than you could imagine. It speaks loudly on what is important, what you are going to pay attention to, and what you expect of the staff.

2. **Maintain a "President's List."** These are jobs that are sufficiently large or otherwise important that winning them would make a significant change to the company. It further emphasizes the focus of business development. I advised one company that was closing in on revenue of $100M but that considered jobs in the range of $10M to $20M as "large." Jobs of that size were not large enough to sustain the growth that it needed and its board expected. It needed to bid at least three or four much larger jobs each year and win one or two of those. A President's list was created with a threshold of $50M for a job to make the list. A threshold of $100M would have been even better. These jobs were reviewed first at any business development meeting, and more time was spent focusing on those leads. The practical effect of focusing on these jobs is obvious, but just as important is the psychological effect on the staff. People pay attention to what the leaders focus on. A good business development person will want to make sure that his leads are on this list. This company had a special name for business development folks who didn't have any leads on this list. They were called "former employees."

30. Turn the sales life cycle on its head

If you are in the business of providing services to the government, you take for granted the government acquisition process. Folks in government frequently ask how they can make government procurements more like commercial procurements. In a commercial procurement, the amount of information exchanged between buyer and seller increases as the buyer gets closer to making the purchase. Consider what happens when you buy a new car. During your first visit to a showroom, you may not want to speak with a salesman. You are still figuring out what kind of car interests you. As you get closer to making the purchase, you engage in more detailed discussions with the salesman about what features the cars have and which are the ones that interest you. When you discuss price and are close to making the purchase, you might even say something like "The dealer on the other side of town offered me a similar car at the same price, but that car had more options."

This is exactly opposite to how the government world works. In government procurements, the contracting officers stop all informal contact with potential bidders as the time for bids draws near.

The chart on the next page illustrates this difference between government and commercial buying.

Knowing that communication will slow down and eventually be cut off, especially at the crucial point right around the time that the request for proposals (RFP) is released, means that you have to use the early stages of the process to sell your solution. Recognizing this, you can use this timeline to your advantage. The company that can persuade the client early that its approach is the best has an obvious advantage. Don't ever sit back and wait for an RFP. When I ask my staff or a client about an upcoming RFP, I hate to hear "We are tracking that." That means that they are being passive. Tracking an RFP is never sufficient. You have to be active. You have to be aggressive and force as much communication as you can as frequently as you can and as early as you can. You need to strive to sell an approach before the acquisition process even begins. That way you can influence the RFP and gain a significant advantage in the bidding.

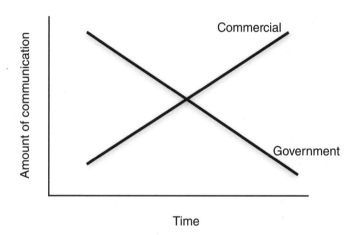

105

31. Don't overbid

There are times when you know more than what is written in an RFP. It is common knowledge to bid to what is in the RFP, not what you know. So why do technical people try to over-engineer a solution? Because that is who they are. Some people call this rule "Don't gold-plate your solution." But this rule is even more fundamental than that. Even if your solution is not gold-plated, it still may be more than what is asked for or what can be awarded. Our experience in bidding a Web portal for the Navy is a good example of where we didn't follow this rule.

A current customer in the Navy was tasked for putting up a Navy-wide Intranet that would serve as a Web portal for sailors. It was under pressure to show that it could get this up and running within 30 days of award, and it made it clear that the winning solution had to have initial capability operational within 30 days. The specifications said that the portal had to support 100,000 simultaneous users. Our technical team said there wasn't any way that they could get a system up and running to support that many users in 30 days. It would take at least twice that long to procure the hardware necessary to support that many users. I explained that the initial system didn't have to have any content. It just had to be a title screen and sign-in screen that our customer could show to its superiors. A PC could handle the expected amount of users, since there weren't going to be many users at first. In fact, there weren't going to be any users at all until we included content in a later release. We would have plenty of time to get all the necessary hardware operational by the time the users came on board. Our technical and proposal writers submitted a solution that required 60 days to be up and running. The customer came back with a deficiency request. It said it needed to have *something* up and running in 30 days. Instead of changing our technical approach, we tried to explain that in 60 days we would have something better.

We lost. The Navy selected a firm that had something running in 30 days, and that contractor eventually built the full portal for the Navy.

This was an exaggerated, obvious case of overbidding. It isn't always so obvious that your solution is more than what it takes to win. As your technical staff develops their solution, it is always a good idea to ask, "What if your customer had only half as much money? What could you still do?" That almost always stimulates some thinking about alternative solutions.

In our Navy portal experience, we also violated another key rule: Don't blow off a government comment.

I've seen other examples where a bidder thought it could explain away a government question with a simple explanation. If the government questions some aspect of your solution, and you are convinced that is still the correct solution and you don't want to change it (usually a bad idea), your explanation needs to be a home run. A short, simple response will not do. Your explanation needs to be more than an explanation; it needs to be so compelling that everyone, even your managers, will see that your approach is the best of *all* possible approaches.

32. Conduct deep-dive lessons learned on all bids, win or lose

Most government agencies will give you useful feedback on a debriefing after a contract is awarded. You should always ask for a debriefing on every bid, whether you won or not. Most companies do a superficial job of recording the reasons why they won or lost. It is important to conduct a formal review and maintain a summary record of the lessons learned.

When they lose, most companies will request a debrief, and, after the debrief, their proposal lead will send a short email to the managers saying something like "We lost on price," or "They liked the other technical solution better," or "We didn't really understand what they wanted." There isn't any mechanism for ensuring that lessons learned influence the next proposal. It is important that a manager conduct a lessons-learned review where folks have a chance to ask questions and discuss what they learned from the government. At SAIC, Dr. Byster, the founder and CEO, sat in on the lessons-learned reviews for every job that they lost.

Most government agencies do a good job of listing the strengths and weaknesses of every major section of your proposal. It is natural to focus on the weaknesses. Identify which weaknesses were a surprise to you. Why did the government see that as a weakness if you didn't? What did you miss?

You should also analyze the listed strengths. Did they point out what you thought you had as strengths? Did they list as a strength something that you didn't even realize was a strength? That has happened more frequently than I ever expected. It is important that you have a mechanism for capturing this feedback so that you can make sure those strengths are part of your next proposal for similar services. Keeping a company memory of strengths is crucial for building a winning proposal-writing organization.

33. Remember the refrigerator light

There is a rule in selling that you have to remember to tell them that the refrigerator light goes out when you close the door. I described in rules 21 and 22 why it is important that your proposals include some idea that an evaluator can call out as a differentiator or strength of your solution. Sometimes that strength doesn't need to be creative or innovative. Sometimes you can get credit for a strength if you describe a fundamental aspect of your solution clearly and fully. I learned this rule recently when a debriefing from a client contained a strength that I was not expecting. The firm described in its proposal how its approach to creating a virtual computer environment would balance a significant decrease in desktop support personnel, with some increase in systems administrators to ensure that there would be significant cost savings while maintaining the proper level of operations. The specifics of this suggestion aren't important. What is important is that we thought that this was a necessary part of everyone's solution. Apparently we explained our solution more fully than the other bidders, and the evaluator identified this as a strength of our solution.

It is important to spell out all of the features and benefits that your approach offers. One way to remember this rule is to remember the refrigerator rule. A woman was shopping for a refrigerator. She went into one store and was interested in a specific model, but she decided to shop some more. A few days later she was in the first store again and the salesman asked if she was still interested in the refrigerator. She said she had bought a similar refrigerator from another store. While both models seemed to have the same features, the one she bought had a feature where the little light inside would go off when she closed the door.

Don't assume that the customer understands all your features and benefits. Make it easy for the customer to recognize and evaluate all your features and benefits, even the obvious ones.

PART THREE
OPERATIONS

34. Projects don't fail for technical reasons

I can imagine that a hardware development could fail because of a bad design, but I've never seen a bad technical design doom an information systems project. I have, of course, seen IT software development projects fail because of a failure to understand the requirements or control the requirements. Building an information technology system requires a different set of processes than building a physical platform, mostly because users don't know what they want until they see it. The management of the development process is what determines its success or failure. When an IT project fails, it is because management failed. The real test of management is how it responds when issues arise or the schedule is at risk. An example of how one company mishandled such a situation is what occurred on a large software development project for the Army Reserve. Coming near to the recompete, it became obvious that the development was behind schedule. The company's CEO overreacted. He removed the Division Director who was over the project and assigned him to replace the Program Manager. The misstep was that the Program Manager on the project was in a key position under the contract, and the company made this change without consultation with the client. Furthermore, the client liked the Program Manager and didn't believe that he or his actions were the cause of the schedule slippage. The schedule issue was not serious, and an agreement could have been reached with open discussion with the client. This wasn't done prior to the personnel changes. Making these changes in the way that they did further annoyed the client. Needless to say, the company lost that recompete. Compare that outcome to what happened when SRA's development of the Defense Property

System ran into schedule and funding issues. The CEO, Renny DiPentima, got personally involved in resolving the issue directly with the Commanding General of TRANSCOM. Working together, they were able to agree on a path forward, and SRA remained the contractor. Open and honest communications with the government saved the project. When a project falls behind schedule, it is the responsibility of management to find out about the issues early and, together with the customer, take action to fix the problem. If the problem isn't fixed to the customer's satisfaction, it is the fault of the managers and the project management process.

35. Combine functional and technical expertise

One characteristic that separated SRA from many of its competitors was that we combined functional and technical expertise on every job and at every step of that job. Some of the more engineering-based companies were used to a project life cycle where functional experts wrote the specifications for whatever they wanted and passed them to technical engineers who would provide the product exactly as specified. SRA grew up in a world where the users didn't know what they want until they saw it. Consequently, we needed to have users, or surrogate users, as an integral part of our team on everything we did. Our work on the modernization of the World Wide Military Command and Control System (WWMCCS) is an example of this principle. In the late 1980s, GTE had a contract to deliver a modernized WWMCCS. After five years, it did not deliver a single working part of the system. The DoD recompeted the contract and SRA won. The story of how we won is a separate lesson, but what is amazing is that we delivered a working system. Under the Joint Operations Planning and Execution System (JOPES) Development and Integrations contract, we delivered the JOPES Core Database, which all command and control applications used for many years. We also delivered working scheduling and movement software that was fielded worldwide. What did we do differently? Since we were used to integrating functional expertise with technical expertise throughout the life cycle, we used functional experts in several ways. We had SRA employees who were former users work with the technical staff side by side in the early stages of development. In that way, these surrogate users could guide the developers, filling in the holes that are an inevitable part of every requirements document. As a software developer would be developing a screen, the surrogate user might say, "You need to have these other data elements on this screen too, even though the specification doesn't call for it. I would need them to do my job."

Once the foundation software was built and we were ready to design user interface screens, we convened a panel of senior "power" users from the government user community. These power users would meet with our developers about once every six weeks to review our proposed screens. We were able to have discussions right then about what was absolutely necessary for the system to work. Our direct customer maintained strict configuration management control of changes, what we needed to change then and what could wait for a later release, and we made the necessary changes before the next user review panel meeting. In this way, when we delivered software, we knew that it would satisfy the users' requirements, not just meet the written specification. We also used our internal functional experts to help us design real-world, scenario-based tests so we tested the system based on how it would be used, not just against the written requirements.

There was a project on which I failed to ensure that we had functional experts integrated with us, and the project subsequently failed because of it. We won a contract to automate a gourmet food store chain in California. We had developed a total, integrated solution for running supermarkets as part of our bid to modernize the Defense Department's commissaries. Some folks in the industry thought that our solution was so good that they recommended that the people at Bristol Farms, a gourmet food chain in California, see a demonstration of it.

At that time, in the 1990s, Bristol Farms stores did not have any automation. They did not have an automated store inventory system, nor did they have automated point-of-sale devices at their check-out counters. We did successfully implement automation in one store, but they then told us that they did not want us under contract any further. This was the only project that I was ever involved in at SRA that was terminated prematurely. It was also the only contract on which we did not have any functional understanding of the requirements. Our solution incorporated a leading product for store inventory that was widely used in the industry. We were relying on experts from that product to be our functional experts. The Bristol Farms executive thought that the software was too conservative, too staid. They wanted something that was more leading-edge. I remember one meeting where we were discussing what we would implement, and the Bristol Farms CIO said he did not want any representatives from that product at the meeting. That meant that we did not have any functional experts advising us. That was a big mistake. We did not have sufficient background to understand what the difference was between products or what we would have to do to implement the system as the Bristol Farms executive suggested. He made several changes to our technical approach, and we did not understand the functional ramifications of those changes. We did get the system implemented, and we did successfully automate their first store, but the relationship did not last. I would not undertake a project again without a functional expert whom I trusted as part of my team.

It doesn't take a lot of functional experts to provide the expertise necessary. One functional expert on the team can easily provide the knowledge necessary for a team of 10 to 15 technical folks to stay on track.

If you are in the government services business, the inclination is for a company to hire experts who used to be in the government. That is fine, but (and it's a big BUT), if you hire a senior person (senior executive service or general officer) make his first year a learning year. Don't give him profit and loss responsibility or a target number to achieve for new business. He won't understand the difference between a real lead and a cup of coffee with a friend. He won't understand the business well enough to make good decisions. Hire senior folks for the strategic value. For functional experts to serve as surrogate users, hire folks from lower levels and integrate them with your project teams in all activities.

36. The business cannot scale linearly (Operations)

As I described above, you can't continue to grow by pursuing only projects of the same size that you pursued when you were small. You cannot reach your growth goals by scaling linearly—that is, by pursuing opportunities that are the same size and type as your current portfolio of projects. Besides needing to bid large jobs to reach your growth goals, there is another reason why you have to pursue ever-larger projects. If you don't, your back-office infrastructure will grow linearly with the business, and the size of the back-office staff will drag down the organization and become unsustainable.

The workload for many back-office functions depends on the number of transactions, not the size of the project or revenue. Contracts and most financial operations are transaction-based operations. It takes just as much effort to process a contract action for $100,000 as it does for a $1M. It takes no more effort to send out an invoice for $1M than it does to send out one for $100,000. The goal for every company needs to be to grow indirect expenses at a slower rate than it is growing revenue. The only way to accomplish that is to continue to add larger projects.

The same rule is true for recruiting. I've found that it is easier to recruit for 40 positions on a new contract than one or two positions. If you win new work with 40 positions, there are efficiencies in recruiting. You can, for example, hold a job fair and attract, interview, and make contingent offers on the spot to a large number of folks at one time. If you are hiring from a previous incumbent contractor, you may be able to work with the customer, advertise the job fair on-site and hold it in a location close to the work site. If you try to fill 10 different jobs with four positions each, it will require a lot more time and resources.

Companies must consciously strive to increase revenue without increasing the size of their back-office staff, or at least have the increase in back-office staff be significantly smaller than the increase in revenue. Tracking the rate of increase of your back-office staff (e.g., HR, Finance, Contracts) and comparing that to the rate of increase of your operating units will give you a good measure of how efficiently you are growing your organization. If a back-office operation is growing at rate near that of an operating unit, then you are headed for a serious financial situation. Eventually your operating expenses will grow to be so large that you will become non-competitive and you will start to lose business. At that point, it may be too late to correct the situation. You have to be watchful of this all of the time. The best way to avoid this problem is to continually win new jobs that are larger than your current ones and require fewer support staff.

37. Track the change in backlog over time

There are many measures of the health of a business. In my consulting practice, I meet many managers who rely only on monthly financial data to keep an eye on the health of the business. These data are important. A manager certainly has to pay attention to cash flow and profit and loss on each project, etc. I've advised many managers who are ignoring one of the most important measures of the health of their business. Even managers who regularly track their backlog do not examine the change in backlog every month. The change in backlog is probably the most important indicator of the health of a business.

A general rule in the government service business is that backlog should be at least two and half times revenue. This is derived from the fact that most contracts are for five years (including options) so at any time, you should have on average two and a half years of backlog. Public companies that are doing well generally report backlog in the range of two and a half to three times annual revenue. Contract lengths are getting shorter, so I expect the normal range for backlog to decrease. If your average contract is three years in length, then a backlog of one and half years would be average. However, the absolute number doesn't tell the story well enough. Consider a small business with $10M/year in revenue that wins a five-year contract for $75M or $15M/year. Its revenue would be at least $25M/year. After two years it still has a backlog of $40M on revenue of $25M. That's not two and a half, but it's not bad either. However, if it went two years without replacing the $30M they used of backlog, it would be in big trouble. At that rate it will be out of business once that contract is over. On the other hand, a company that has had declining backlog for a few years followed by a few years of increasing backlog might be in good shape even if the backlog did not meet the two and half times standard. You have to consider the change in backlog when evaluating the amount of backlog and the health of a business.

If you are going several quarters without replacing the backlog that you have converted to revenue, you are on a downward curve regardless of your financial results. That is why I recommend to all businesses, small and large, that they manage their pipeline so that they bid at least one large (whatever "large" means to them) job each quarter. If you have an average win rate on large jobs of around 30 percent then you should win at least one large job a year. Very large businesses will have to bid more than one large job a quarter. You should analyze your pipeline this way: If you win your expected percentage, will you win enough new business to compensate for how much your backlog will decrease from execution? For most small and mid-sized businesses, one win a year that significantly increases the backlog is sufficient. Large businesses will need more.

The change in backlog is so important that at SRA we gave this measure equal weight to revenue and margin in the performance plans of senior managers. At the beginning of each fiscal year, goals were established for senior managers. Each senior manager was given three goals of almost equal weight. These goals were based on revenue for the year, gross margin for the year, and a target based on new awards that was set so as to measure the increase in the backlog. If, going into a fiscal year, a division had a backlog of $50M and the growth targets each year were 10 percent growth, then the division's goal for new awards would be set so that it would finish the year with a 10 percent increase in backlog, or $55M. This would set up the division for 10 percent growth the following year.

Some companies and analysts measure this as the "book to bill ratio." Are you booking new work at a greater rate than you are billing for your current work? If you are not increasing the amount of your business, then you are in trouble.

38. Shine a light

If you want to improve something, shine a light on it. Make it the focus of reviews. I think this lesson is well-known, but it is so important that it is worth emphasizing. As a manager, you can't put the same emphasis on everything at the same time. Pick those items that need improvement most and make sure the staff sees that those are the items that will get your attention.

When our Days Sales Outstanding (DSOs, a measure of cash-flow) increased, we saw that we needed to do a better job of getting large invoices out faster. Our invoicing manager posted each day, on each invoicing person's door, the invoices that each person sent out that day. It created a little competition among the invoicing team. They didn't like that, but they did get the invoices out faster.

There are many techniques for shining a light. You can create a management dashboard where you regularly review the key metrics from your organization. If you do create such a dashboard, make sure that every manager has visibility into the results. You need to make this information visible to all the managers you want to influence. You should also bring up the topics that need attention at your regular review or weekly meetings. Make sure that everyone gets the message that a particular topic is important to you and that they will be evaluated on those results.

When my organization has fallen down in some area, shining a light on that area and making it visible to everyone has always brought positive results.

39. Remember your place

The service business is a relationship-based business, and relationships are an important key to growing a business. However friendly you are with your customers, they are not your friends. The fact that you are in a client-contractor relationship will not be forgotten by the client. Be especially careful in what appears to be a social situation, such as after hours at a conference. You are always in a business setting. As a manager, you need to teach your staff this lesson. It is inevitable that some of your folks will become friends with some of the government staff. They need to understand that regardless of their personal relationship, there is a line that they cannot cross.

I've made a point in this book that a successful contractor will give advice to its customer. You should do that, but you have to make it positive, don't lecture the customer. Your style is the key. This is especially difficult for some senior folks who are recently retired from the government. I know of at least one situation where a senior manager was attending a meeting with several customers present. The senior manager began to tell the customer, in strong language, what it was doing wrong. One of the key government managers got tired of being lectured on what he should be doing, got up from the table, said, "I don't have to take this anymore," and walked out. Needless to say, when the recompete came up, the company lost.

Remember your place. Always maintain a professional demeanor.

40. Project kick-off determines project success

Soon after I arrived at TechTeam, we started a project for the General Services Administration's Public Building Service. This project quickly got into trouble. It became obvious that the project could not be completed on schedule. The project team did not understand the customer's fundamental problem. The project looked on the surface to be a help desk project, but it was really a system development/system integration project. Later the project manager admitted that he hadn't even read the proposal. He had no idea what the real requirements were, nor did he understand what we had committed to. We realized that this was a systems integration project when it was too late. Had we held a substantive kick-off meeting our project team could have discovered what the real requirements were early enough to put the right resources on the project. At SRA, we started a form of kick-off meeting (called "Go-Team") that was designed to focus on just these questions: Do we understand the requirements? Do we have the right resources to kick off the project? The concept was a good one that, if followed, could help a project stay out of trouble.

The time for senior managers to discover what resources a project needs to succeed is at the start of the project, not after it turns bad.

41. Reorganize, but do it quickly

Don't be afraid to reorganize, but don't drag it on. Most managers spend a lot of time fretting over a reorganization of their business. They worry that the staff won't accept the new organization, or they worry that work will come to a standstill as everyone adjusts. Everyone has seen examples where, once discussions of a pending reorganization start, works slows down as everyone speculates and gossips about what they think might happen. Sometimes this goes on for months. Because we have all observed this happening, we become frozen and skittish about starting any talk of reorganizing, even when we know that one is needed. The trick is to do it quickly and communicate frequently with all employees through multiple channels. Once you decide that a reorganization is useful to the business, quickly develop your alternatives, socialize the approach with the senior managers with whom you are comfortable sharing this information, and quickly make your decision on what the new organization will be and who will be the leaders in each position. Then quickly communicate the changes and reasons for the changes to the staff. Ensure that your managers understand the reasons for the change so they can answer questions from their staff. The folks will adjust if it is done quickly and explained well. People like to know who is in charge and who is responsible for what. Once the uncertainty is gone, business will quickly go back to normal. Keep the time of uncertainty to a minimum and everything will work out fine.

42. Choose an organizing principle that fits your business model

Organizations spend as much time discussing how they should be organized as they spend on any other management topic. There are several paradigms for the major organizational principle: You can organize around:

1. Customer

2. Specialty or skill set, which can be either a functional or technical skill

3. Geography

You should choose one of these overriding structures and establish rules for dealing with the overlap with the other two. Disputes among organizations are worse when there is a mix of principles. If one business unit thinks it owns a customer and another business owns all work in a skill area, then a conflict between the two business units is inevitable. SRA, like most other companies, tried various models of organizing around customers or specialties over the years. Also like other companies, we never had a pure model that avoided these types of conflicts. Since we are a customer-focused business, I've found that the most efficient organizing principle is to organize around customer communities. It is possible that an organization can be formed around both skills and customers at the same time. For example, if one skill area is software development and another is base operations, then you will generally be selling these to different customers anyway. I'll describe what I mean by selling to customer communities, and then I will describe ways of dealing with the overlap with specialties and geographies.

I use the phrase "customer communities" rather than just "customers" because there are some natural affiliations between customers that may not be obvious at first. When I organized the Defense Systems division into Strategic Business Units, the question came up of where our work for the Military Sealift Command (MSC) and the Army Military Traffic Management Command (MTMC, now SDDC) should be placed in our organization. Should our MTMC work, as an Army command, be in the same organization as our Army business or should it be in the organization with our other transportation work under the joint command, U. S. Transportation Command (TRANSCOM)? MTMC is an Army organization, but it is also a component command of TRANSCOM. What mattered to me is that TRANSCOM, MTMC, MSC, and AMC (Air Mobility Command) all participated in the same organization: the National Defense Transportation Association (NDTA). It didn't make sense to send three or four business development folks to every NDTA lunch or conference. Rather, it was more efficient to have one business development person responsible for this "community." Therefore, I put all the components of this community in one business unit.

As I mentioned before, a company needs to have specialties. Sometimes it is not practical for every business unit to have the resources to be expert in all of a company's specialties. Especially when developing new skills, you will not have the resources to develop these skills in every division. I'll describe a few ways that this can be handled successfully.

For some specialties, we created a division of Offerings and Solutions. This was a cost center, not a profit center. All the revenue that this center generated was counted in one of the customer-facing business units. Of course, data on revenue and profit were maintained for each of the specialties to ensure that the investment had an appropriate return. Establishing a division or center that contains offerings and solutions does require an investment, but this is the best approach, especially for those specialties that are highly specialized and require money for training and to maintain a close relationship with the vendor. It avoided any territorial dispute.

It is also possible to assign a specialty to a business unit that has profit and loss responsibility, but it is important that that business unit understands that its role in managing the specialty is a corporate responsibility to help other business units, not just to generate revenue for itself. Frequently a specialty will first appear in a business unit as an outgrowth of a current project. For example, one business unit will be the first to need trained experts in a product such as VMWare or a business intelligence product such as Cognos. It may not make sense for every business unit to invest in training its people in these tools. It will be more efficient to centralize the training and vendor relationship. Keeping this special skill centralized in a P&L unit can work, but only if it is managed as if it were a corporate resource when that skill is needed by another division. Revenue should be recorded by the customer-oriented business unit with a form of credit given to the supporting division. At SRA we allowed the unit that owned the specialty to also double-count the revenue, but this does add complexity to financial forecasting. Regardless of how this is handled, incentives must be established for all units to cooperate with each other.

One example of a specialty that remained in just one business unit but serviced the other business units was a specialized economic analysis that existed in our Civil Government division. I had a need for this expertise from time to time, but I didn't see this as a core part of our defense business at the time. Therefore I was content to obtain that expertise from Civil when I needed it. Had I seen this as a skill that was essential to our growth in Defense, it would have been the responsibility of the Civil business to ensure that our Defense folks became trained and self-sufficient in that skill over time.

It is important to recognize that some specialties have a life cycle where they may start in a business unit as a specialty that services others, but as the need for that specialty becomes more universal, each business unit may need to have its own internal expertise and support, and that specialty should no longer be centrally managed. For example, when SRA first started doing software development, all programmers and database designers were in one organization. This did make training more efficient and allowed us to develop a consistent company approach to software development. However, we knew that as we grew, every division would need to manage a workforce of software developers, and that specialty eventually evolved to being a skill set that everyone had.

For some years SRA employed a matrix organization that contained all software development staff and later all technical staff. I'll describe how this matrix organization worked and how it evolved over time.

SRA's Software Development Group. In the late 1980s, SRA was still a relatively small company ($25-$100M) that wanted to grow into a large company building large systems. Most of the projects that we had that required us to develop software solutions were small projects of five or six software development folks led by a project manager who was an expert in the functional area of the application. These project managers were not technical people, although they were managing technical projects. They were people who were formerly with the customer community. They had the understanding of the problem and knew which solutions would work well and which wouldn't. While this was a good approach to developing small systems, the technical staff were not feeling fulfilled in their work. Having the technical staff work for a project manager whose background was not technical created some issues that I'll describe below.

At this same time, the Department of Defense was starting to put some emphasis on the work of the Software Engineering Institute (SEI) in evaluating the software capabilities of a com-

pany. This emphasis included evaluating the level of standardiza-
tion of the processes and procedures that a company used on its
various projects. This work eventually became the SEI's Capability Maturity Model and its associated evaluations.

SRA faced two distinct problems associated with its software development projects. On the one hand, we wanted to establish common software development processes so we would
score high on the SEI's evaluation. On the other hand, we needed
a better model for the career development of our technical staff.
The people on our small projects did not like the situation where
their manager was the functional project manager. There were
several reasons for this. They did not see opportunities for advancement, since their project manager was generally not eager
to see them move to another project even it was for a promotion.
They also didn't see their PM as their role model for their career
advancement. They wanted to work for a senior technical leader
who could give them career advice, who they felt could better
evaluate their performance, and who could help them move on
to other projects when the time was right for them. Our answer
to help both of these situations was to create a matrix organization of software development professionals that we named the
Software Development Group, SDG. Emerson Thompson became the Director of SDG and I became the Deputy Director.
SDG had responsibility for the technical execution of software
development projects, for people management of software developers, and for establishing standard processes that would be evaluated at Level 3 of the SEI Capability Maturity Model. Of course
the Project Managers and business unit leaders did not like this
arrangement. They did not like losing control of resources that
were necessary to fulfilling their responsibility. Emerson and I
had to work constantly to demonstrate that we would do whatever we had to do to ensure successful completion of their projects.

The SDG matrix organization worked very well for several years as we grew. We eventually added systems engineers
and other technical folks to the matrix organization. SDG did

accomplish its goals. We did rate high on the SEI's Capability Maturity Model. We established a workable solution to moving people from one project to another in a way that didn't cause undue harm to any one project while helping to advance people's careers. When the business units grew large enough to support the technical staff in these ways on their own, SDG was dissolved and the technical folks were moved into the business units.

However, there was one role that SDG performed that we kept In the Business Units. We created in the business units a position for someone to be a "staffing" director. We wanted to maintain a structure available to folks when they felt that they needed to get off of a project for their career advancement. These staffing directors would also be responsible for placing people when a project ended or folks were no longer needed on a project. Based on our experience with matrix organization, we believed that this would work better if these staffing directors worked for the business unit manager rather than Human Resources. SRA might have been the only company that had people within the business units dedicated solely to helping people find other projects throughout the company. In most companies, when a person lands on the bench he is directed to a list of vacancies and told that he could apply for those positions. In some companies, the résumés of folks on the bench go into the same pile as the résumés from people outside the company who are applying for advertised positions. We wanted a staff dedicated to helping people with their careers. Staffing directors existed in some form at least until I left the company in 2006.

The matrix organization worked well while we were a midsized company, but as we grew it was more efficient to operate with strict line organizations. However, the residual staffing organization helped both the people and the business and became a differentiator for the company.

43. Operate as one company

In addition to bidding as one company as I discussed in Rule 24, it is important to operate as one company. Many companies talk about doing that. Unfortunately, in many companies business units do not cooperate with one another. I learned early on in my time at SRA that non-cooperation was not acceptable behavior. I joined SRA in 1983 to work on a very large new project. Our project was one of the first to have a personal computer, which was then an IBM PC. Our project occupied an entire corner of our building space. The PC was set up in the hallway so several of us could use it. I recall a time when someone from another project came over to our area to use "our" PC. One of the senior people on our project told that person that he couldn't use "our" PC. Ted Legasey, SRA's COO, overheard that conversation and publicly chastised our person. I remember his words clearly. He made it clear that such behavior was unacceptable. He warned that if that was the attitude of this project, he would "cut off this end of the building and let it drift away." He would not tolerate such an attitude. That left quite an impression on me as a new employee. I still hear examples from other companies where one business unit won't let employees from another business unit use "their" soda machine. A company needs to work hard to make sure that organization lines don't create barriers.

Why is this so important? I found that operating as one company gave us a true advantage in both bidding and execution. Operating as one company meant more than just playing nice with each other or allowing folks to move from one business unit to another. It meant that the processes we used to manage and execute a project were the same in every organization. For project management, everyone attended the same training, everyone used the same financial system, and everyone followed the same templates for monthly project reviews. During software development, everyone followed the same development processes. When we won the contract for the U.S. Agency for International Development (USAID), this single approach was a key to our successful execution. This was the largest single project we had ever started. Out of necessity, we drew from staff from all across the organization. We had employees who had worked only on civil government projects, on defense-only projects, and employees who came out of the intelligence community. What was important was that we didn't have to spend (waste) any time training people on how we wanted to manage the project. The format for financial reports, monthly progress reports, and risk management were already known by all of our task leads, regardless of their background.

In order for this to work, senior management needs to emphasize working as one company as a key part of the corporate culture. When I became COO at SRA, I put a lot of emphasis on our 1SRA initiative. I know of many companies that have this type of initiative, but few carry out that promise. Company leadership has to be serious about enforcing standards among operating units. There has to be one project management course, one set of standards and procedures, and one set of financial reporting formats that everyone follows. Even more important, there has to be a culture where people are encouraged to work on projects that are in different divisions. Senior management must put in place incentives that reinforce this behavior and disincentives for those that do not exhibit it. That is the hard part of implementing a one-company approach, and that can't work without true senior management commitment.

I don't believe that we could have had such a successful start on our USAID project without this unified approach.

44. Who rules?

There are two fundamentally different approaches to running a business. Either the business units have the final decision-making authority, or the support units, such as finance and accounting, have that authority. In most companies that I've worked with it is the business unit, but not in all companies. When Logicon existed as a separate company, we were a subcontractor to it on a major ID/IQ contract. Much of our work for the Defense Information Systems Agency (DISA) was coming up for recompete under that contract. We knew that having the low price was going to be very important. On the first task orders that came out, we asked Logicon to keep its load on us to less than 10 percent. The Logicon business manager agreed with me. He really wanted to win this business, and he was incentivized to capture that revenue. He also knew that if the load was much higher, we wouldn't be competitive. Their pricing person, however, reported to the CFO, not to the business manager. He said he was interested in the work only if the load was close to 17 percent. After a lot of discussions, the pricing person held his ground. There wasn't anything that the business unit VP could do. We lost that task, and eventually lost all of our work because of price.

The business units with profit-and-loss responsibility should have the final decision-making responsibility, but regardless of how you choose to run your business, it must be crystal clear who has the deciding vote.

45. Remember your field sites

Sooner or later, you will want to expand outside of your headquarter's geographic area. Once you begin to have employees in distant cities, management takes on a new and different responsibility. Every person who works outside of the city where the company headquarters is located feels that the company is out of touch with him. He feels neglected, and believes that he is not hearing the same amount of corporate information as folks in the HQ. Whether this is true or not, this is how folks outside your HQ feel. In order to keep these employees engaged and feeling a part of the company, there are several techniques that you can use.

Copy the role of a military installation commander: When you have multiple projects in a remote or field location that report to different divisions, it is common that these projects do not coordinate well and the people in those locations do not feel attached to one another or to the company. When I consult to companies in this situation, I recommend that they follow the model of how the military deals with multiple commands on the same installation.

One senior person is designated as the regional lead or "site commander." That person is responsible for the caring of all employees in that area or office. He is responsible for the morale and welfare of the employees regardless of which business unit they are from. That means he conducts all-hands meetings with everyone, has responsibility for communications between the corporation and remote staff, and needs to do whatever is necessary to support the employees. For example, if the company is holding a holiday party, it is the site commander's responsibility to ensure that the event includes everyone in that location. The site commander functions in this role as a senior corporate manager, not as a division director.

Frequent visits by headquarters staff: In the mid-1990s, SRA won a contract to provide IT support to the Navy at the Puget Sound Naval Shipyard outside Seattle. The company that had the contract previously was also headquartered in the Washington, D.C. area. That company let the project be run entirely by its local office. Senior managers from the company's headquarters never even visited the work site at the shipyard. That might seem like a welcome approach. The managers of that project might have liked the fact that they were left alone, but that had negative consequences. When SRA won the job, we hired all the employees of the previous contractor. Sometime later that year, I visited with our employees and the customer at Puget Sound. I was the third SRA Vice President to visit the customer and our employees on-site since we won the contract. The customer told me that he was happy to see that his project was getting such great attention from SRA's executives. He said that no one from the HQ of the previous contractor ever visited him or his employees the entire time that he held the contract. He went to say that while he liked the employees on-site, he didn't see any value from the company overall, and we won the contract precisely because the customer was hoping to receive added value from a company.

It is important that HQ show their support for a project, but it is also important that HQ not try to micro-manage the project. The customer and our employees valued our support, but the customer also wanted the project manager to have a high degree of authority and to be able to act quickly when necessary. The approach has to be that a company's headquarters and its staff support the project rather than manage it.

Plan for Morale and Welfare (M&W) activities in your budget. When you hold activities near your HQ such as a holiday party, summer picnic, or a summer group visit to a baseball game, you should always budget for your field sites to have a similar activity. Consider these expenses as part of your annual budget process and create a separate line item for field site M&W.

46. Early reports are wrong

Early reports are frequently wrong, but they are always incomplete. We know this is true when describing many news events. The first reports on 9/11 said a twin-engine prop plane had accidentally hit one of the World Trade Center Towers. On Election Day 2004, the first reports of exit polls said John Kerry was winning. I first learned this rule from my colleagues who had fought in wars. This principle was well-known to them. Many people would go further and say, "Early reports always contain something that is inaccurate, if not flat-out entirely wrong." Some people teach that the first report is always wrong. A lot of managers don't understand that this rule applies to business too. Wayne Blackburn taught me this lesson. Wayne was the Deputy Director of Defense Systems at SRA when I was the Director. Wayne would be the conduit for how I first heard about a personnel or other serious problem. Before I could jump to a conclusion, Wayne would remind me of this rule. Following his guidance, I would gather further information before making a decision.

This rule applies to all aspects of business. When you lose a job, don't jump to an assumption of why you lost. Wait for the debriefing. When you are told that a system you are developing is behind schedule, the first reason you are given is never the full story.

This rule is especially applicable when it comes to personnel problems. As we have been taught, there is always a second side to any story. There isn't just a second side; usually the facts change as you conduct further investigations. There is always some aspect of the situation that wasn't clear to us when we first heard it. Don't jump to a conclusion. Unless you absolutely have to make a decision on first reports during a crisis, wait for clarifications and more information. They will almost always give you additional relevant information on which to make decisions.

PART FOUR
TALENT
MANAGEMENT

47. Build a trust bank

Many managers are hesitant to present negative information to employees. They try to sugar-coat what they have to say when conveying information that they know employees will not like. The way to deal with negative information is to first build a trust bank. Ted Legasey, SRA's COO for most of its history, taught me this lesson. He was thoroughly committed to dealing with all employees in a straightforward, honest manner all the time. He taught me that if you are always forthright and honest with employees, they will accept bad news more easily. If you build up deposits in your trust bank, you can draw on that trust when presenting bad news. Ted made a point of answering every question asked at an all-hands meeting in the most direct way possible. He taught that those were opportunities to build up your trust bank. Then, when you had to deliver news that employees wouldn't like, they knew that you were telling them the whole story and could better understand your reasons for your decision. People appreciate it when they are told the complete reasons behind an unpopular decision. I always admired the way Ted handled these situations. I think this was a key part of SRA's culture under Ted, and I tried to emulate that behavior as much as possible.

Most of the managers in a company don't realize how little their employees trust them. There exists a natural skepticism about authority that is the default attitude of many employees. You have to work diligently to overcome that feeling of distrust. Make deposits in your trust bank as frequently as possible.

48. Hire for attitude, train for skills

I don't recall where I first heard this, but it is a good principle to manage by. It is difficult, however, to identify the characteristics of attitude that will make for good employees and include those characteristics in your hiring and employee evaluation processes. Ted Legasey, SRA's first COO, identified five characteristics that every employee must possess or he will not be an employee for long. These characteristics served as a basis for evaluating every employee. The ideal situation would be if all of our new hires had these characteristics:

- Integrity. Integrity is knowing the difference between right and wrong, caring about that difference, and doing something about it.

- Strong work ethic. This is not measured by how many hours a person works. Rather, it means "I care about the quality of my work."

- Positive attitude. We all know that one person with a negative attitude can ruin a project. If someone does not have a positive attitude, you don't want him on your team.

- Intelligence. This doesn't mean high IQ. It means being smart, but always wanting to learn more.

- Substantive expertise. This is what is on a person's résumé. A person needs to be good at something.

The first four characteristics are attitudes. Only the fifth reflects skills. If someone has these five characteristics, he can be trained for new skills as technical positions require. If you ignore the four attitude characteristics, you might have a good employee in the short run, but you will not have the staff needed to sustain a thriving company. These characteristics were taught to every employee by Ted Legasey. They form the perfect foundation for evaluating employees.

49. Manage to people's strengths

It is extremely rare to find an individual who is very good at everything you want him or her to do. While most managers understand this, they still frequently hire and manage while expecting every employee to be good at everything. If you can find someone who excels at a skill you need and don't otherwise have, then you need to create a role for that person on your team. An obvious example is where you have a technical person whom you absolutely need to get a job done, but that person is horrible at managing people. You could create a technical lead position that doesn't require direct people supervision.

It doesn't matter whether we are talking about a project team or a management team. You may need to make adjustments to your organization to take advantage of people's strengths. Frequently this won't mean that the organization structure needs to change; rather, it will mean that whom you put in each role may depend on whom else you have in a position. When I was appointed as Director of Defense Systems at SRA, Ted Legasey and Renny DiPentima recognized that the best use of my skills to help grow the defense business was to pair me with a deputy who could let me spend a great deal of time outside the office with customers and prospective customers. I was told that Wayne Blackburn would be my deputy. Usually, a company lets a new director select his deputy, but Ted and Renny weren't taking any chances. Wayne and I had worked together on a major project where we had an acrimonious relationship. Everyone who knew us was surprised that we could work as a team, because of our history. Ted and Renny, however, recognized that a Kriegman-Blackburn pair was the right combination to run the business unit. We had just the right set of complementary skills that the business unit needed. We worked together as one of the best director/deputy pairs that I have ever seen. During our seven years together, the Defense Systems business grew from $48M a year in revenue to over $400M. People at SRA still tell me that we are the role model for effective division leadership. In addition to our mutual respect for the other's abilities, we became close friends. The success of the Defense Systems business unit and my personal success are due in large part to Wayne and the decision to put us together.

I am frequently asked by CEOs to evaluate the skills and potential of their leadership team. I stress that this review requires more than just evaluating individuals. You have to evaluate people in the context of the role that they are in and consider the role that they should be in. Having your folks in the right seat on the bus is just as important as getting the right folks on the bus.

50. Move people around

Organization lines create boundaries that can be barriers to creating a single culture and operating as a single company. This can also lead to a group-think mentality that doesn't welcome new ideas. Don't let folks get too attached to whatever organization just happens to be in place at any time. Identify the up-and-coming leaders and ensure that they get exposed to all facets of the business. One large company that I know used corporate staff positions as a means to expose employees to the entire company. They would identify key people and put them in a position such as Director of Corporate Quality Assurance for a year. In that way, they would get exposed to parts of the company that they otherwise wouldn't have had any contact with. They would learn how other divisions work and have an opportunity to interact with corporate leaders at all levels. When they returned to their home division, they were better trained in how the company wanted them to think and behave.

You should consider instituting a regular program for moving people around. Examples of these moves:

- Move people between business development and operations

- Move people between operations and staff roles, such as Quality Development

- Move people between operating units—for example, between civil government and Department of Defense projects

Moving people around helps breaks down organizational barriers and biases and gets people to think in terms of what is good for the entire company and not just their division. Some level of competition between operating units can be good, but when people identify themselves more with their operating unit than with the company, this competition becomes destructive and hinders the growth of the business. By moving people around, you ensure that everyone understands that the company is the only organization that really counts.

51. Fit all employees into your vision

Many employees do not understand how they contribute to the vision of the company. Either the vision is not clear or it is narrow and doesn't cover all of the current work of a company. Ensuring that all employees understand how they fit into the corporate vision to help the company achieve its goals is one of the key characteristics in creating an engaged workforce.

For most of SRA's history, we did a great job in this area. The company vision was clear, and everyone understood how they were contributing to our growth in accordance with our vision. But there was a time when we lost that focus. For a period of time, SRA's senior managers focused almost exclusively on growing a commercial business. We were in the early stages of preparing for a public offering. We believed that by our growing a commercial business, Wall Street analysts would place a greater value on our company. At a corporate off-site for senior staff, only commercial work was discussed. The mid-level managers at the off-site understood what the company was trying to accomplish by growing a commercial practice, but it wasn't easy explaining to the staff, who were mostly working on government contracts. When we returned from the off-site everyone wanted to know what was discussed and what was the corporate focus and direction. We couldn't say that we discussed only commercial work. That would only have confused them and certainly would not have motivated them.

Every employee wants to feel that he is contributing to the company in an important way. Whether you are developing a vision statement, a strategic plan, or an annual message to all employees, make sure that all employees can see how they fit in to the company's plans. I see vision statements that are narrow and exclude some of their current work and the contributions of current employees. For example, I see vision statements that focus on software development or other technical work or system development. In many of these cases, the company has significant analytical work, perhaps data analysis or consulting work. When that happens, you are sending a message to some of your employees that they don't matter. You need to take every action to avoid this perception. Consider all of your work and all of your employees when you address all-hands meetings, when you write your newsletter, and when you conduct your awards and recognitions program. Your employees do pay attention to your vision. Use it to motivate and drive performance. Don't unintentionally alienate a segment of your population.

52. Reward results, not effort

While it should be obvious that it is results that should be rewarded, all too often it is effort that is rewarded, or, even worse, rewards are distributed almost uniformly among the staff. Reward top performers much more than average performers. This was obvious to me for many years, and I never thought about a company doing it any other way. After I left SRA, I joined a company that had just acquired a small, privately owned company. That company had a bonus-system philosophy that is common in small companies but doesn't work for large ones. Nearly everyone in that company received an annual bonus. To some employees this seemed like a very good idea. It was not, however, a good idea to the outstanding employees. As with every company, there was a limited, fixed bonus pool. By giving a bonus to nearly everyone, there was not sufficient money to properly reward the truly outstanding folks who were responsible for bringing in the business. The top performers saw that folks who didn't contribute to the company's growth received almost as much bonus as they did. The top performers soon left the company, leaving only those employees who were glad that everyone got a bonus. That drove the company to mediocrity, not superior performance. A top-tier company will always find ways to reward top performers much better than the average performers, and giving out bonuses carefully to the top-tier folks is a characteristic of top-performing companies.

Likewise, rewarding effort alone will dilute the bonus pool and leave less money for those whose contributions resulted in driving the company's success.

Rewards are not just in the form of bonuses. They also come in the form of salary increases. Many supervisors understand that when it comes to bonuses, you reward results, but they will fail to follow this rule when it comes to salary increase. If you set an average salary increase of say, 4 percent for the year, then your supervisors will set increases in such a way that most employees will receive 4 percent increases and almost everyone will be within a point or two of the average. What happens over time is that the really outstanding new employees will never make as much as an average employee who just happens to have more years of experience. This is not the effect that you want. This is the problem of salary convergence. You need an approach where the outstanding employees will quickly be able to receive higher salaries than the average employee in the same skill area. In order to accomplish this, you need to have a much greater standard deviation around the average than most managers are comfortable with. If you create some simple graphs showing salaries over time, the convergence problem becomes obvious. If the salaries of your outstanding young employees are not on a trajectory to overtake the salaries of your more senior average employees in a reasonable amount of time, you will likely lose those employees to other companies.

Related to this rule is the fact some technical folks have skills that are so rare and critical that their salaries are greater than those of their managers. This is sometimes a difficult situation for managers to accept, but you have to pay people at their market value.

If your compensation also includes stock shares or stock options, it is even easier to take your eye off the ball in that area. After a few years of including stock options with your compensation packages for senior folks, you can easily get out of sync between who has the most options and who are the most valuable employees. You need to look at that every year and make sure that you normalize and compensate for performance and future value to the company, not just longevity.

Tracking salary convergence is a necessary part of good management. Unless you track projected salaries every year, your compensation system will quickly get out of hand.

53. Money doesn't motivate

I'm referring here to relatively small spot bonuses. Most companies have some program for rewarding rank-and-file employees with a spot bonus, usually in an amount between $100 and $1,000. Almost every supervisor, manager, and employee that I've asked has said that he thinks the best way to offer this type of bonus is as cash. Chester Elton, co-author of *The Carrot Principle*, taught me that this is the worst way to give a spontaneous reward. Studies have shown that when employees are asked what they did with their bonus, the most frequent answer is "Paid my bills." The second most frequent response is "I don't remember." The cash just went into their checking accounts. This type of reward has very little lasting motivating affect.

The ideal reward would be to give a gift that you know the person would like to receive. Perhaps it is a large-screen TV. Imagine a visitor to his or her house commenting on the TV and the employee replies, proudly, "My company gave that to me." Or perhaps an X-box or iPad would be the perfect gift.

If you give a gift, make sure that you adjust the amount in your accounting system so the employee does not have to pay income tax on the value of the gift. If giving a gift is not practical, then gift cards are a good second choice. That forces them to buy something rather than putting the cash in the bank and forgetting about it. Again, remember to adjust the amount in the accounting system so you can give them a gift card as a "net" amount.

When I became COO at SRA, I learned that an office manager at a field site was receiving an annual bonus of $500 and that that had been the practice for several years. I had no problem with that person getting a bonus of $500, but I asked the manager, Why only an annual bonus? Usually annual bonuses were larger. The manager explained that the office manager put in extra hours setting up a conference several times a year and this was her reward and recognition. It would have been much better to reward her work at the end of each conference rather than once a year. The bonus coming at the end of the year would not have the same effect. It was probably perceived more as "This is December, so I get an extra $500." It would have been much better if after a conference the manager said, "You worked hard and extra hours making this a successful conference. For your contributions, here is a gift certificate for you and your husband to have dinner at your favorite restaurant."

Spot bonus programs can be a useful program for rewarding employees, but it will be more meaningful if the bonuses are in the form of gifts rather than cash. Welcomed, long-lasting gifts have a long-lasting motivating affect.

54. Manage careers, not projects

One of the most common reasons why incumbents lose their current work is that their costs have gotten out of line with market prices. Their people became overpriced for the work they were doing. If someone is on a project for five years, doing the same job, and doing it well, he will almost certainly become overpaid for the skills required for that job. Especially in the information technology area, you can usually hire a new college graduate to perform the technical work for less money than someone with experience will cost. If your staff has been getting regular salary increases without progressing in their careers or learning new skills, they are almost certainly overpaid compared to what is needed for those skills. The approach to avoiding this predicament is to help people advance in their careers. Usually this means moving staff off of projects where they are well liked by the customer and moving them to a project where they will have more responsibility. In order to keep the customer satisfied, you need an orderly process for ensuring that the replacement person is in place and acceptable to the customer before moving someone off of the project. This requires a lot of planning and frequent communication with your customer. While customers never like their good people to be moved off of their projects, I've found that if this is presented as a career opportunity for the individual, rather than just something to help the company, the customer will accept it. Of course if you can promote someone to more responsibility within the project, that makes everyone happy.

If you hire someone for the long term, not just the project at hand, you should pay some attention to making sure that their careers are progressing. Emerson Thompson, my first manager at

SRA, taught me a long time ago that you want to make sure that you get 10 years of experience, not one year of experience 10 times. While every person needs to be responsible for his own career, companies should realize that they have a responsibility in this area too. There are very practical business reasons for this. Managing a person's career will help the company stay competitive.

55. Foster loyalty to the company, not a person

You need to foster a culture where people are loyal to the company, not to an individual. All of the above ideas are geared to reaching this goal. It is all too common in our industry to have a key individual leave and take several key folks with him. Frequently the folks who leave are the up-and-coming next generation of leaders that the company is depending on for its sustained growth. Operating as one company, rewarding results, having everyone understand that taking care of employees is a company priority, all help establish this company loyalty. If you find a supervisor who doesn't fit this model, one who resists moving his staff to other projects, for example, that person must be trained and evaluated to behave differently. Otherwise he will put the enterprise in jeopardy. One of the reasons that companies forget about this lesson is that they focus on a related lesson: folks quit their supervisor, not a company. That is generally true, and it is important to have supervisors trained so that people like working for them. They are the day-to-day face of the company. However, the supervisor has to leverage the relationship with employees in such a manner that the employees understand what the company is doing for them.

PART FIVE
MERGERS AND ACQUISITIONS

How do you make acquisitions work?

Many acquisitions are not considered successful. Sometimes the reason for the failure is that the company doesn't fully consider how it is going to complete integration. Once you decide to acquire a company, the work begins to make the integration work. Let me repeat, integration begins when you make the decision to acquire a company. You can't wait until the transaction is complete to tackle the integration issues. I was part of the acquisition process at four different companies with different approaches to acquisition. I am also advising companies where M&A is part of their strategy. Sooner or later, every company becomes interested in either acquiring another business or selling theirs. Your approach to M&A needs to be flexible since every acquisition comes with its own set of opportunities and issues. There are, however, some lessons learned that can help make the process smoother.

56. Don't assume you understand their business model

Different companies have different business models. The relationship between revenue and margin is not the same in all lines of business. The compensation models may be different as well. People assume that if they are acquiring a company that appears to be in the same business as they are, the business models must be the same. That isn't true.

When SRA acquired Touchstone Corporation I hadn't yet learned this lesson. Our business, like most government service providers, operates under a model where most people either work directly on a project or are indirect staff. Indirect staff includes full-time managers as well as the business development, finance, accounting, and HR staff. Some folks might be directly billable for only a portion of their time, but by and large, most people are planned to be entirely one or the other. Most folks in fact are planned to work on projects and are on indirect only when they are between projects, that is, "on the bench." Sometimes an unforeseen circumstance happens and a large group of employees are on the bench. This could be the result of losing a recompete or a project is put on hold waiting for additional funding. In any event, as soon as it is known that a number of folks unexpectedly hit the bench, you can predict the impact on your indirect budget. You can then take steps to mitigate that impact by, for example, reducing the training budget for that quarter, or reducing conference attendance or travel. By keeping close track of your list of folks on the bench, you can get an early warning to negative impacts on your indirect costs in sufficient time to offset those effects.

Touchstone, however, was a different business model. It was the classic consulting business where everyone charged some of their time direct and some of it indirect. That is, everyone was able to charge some of their time to a project, but most employees also charged some of their time to company overhead, not to a specific project. When a project was short of money or otherwise could not cover everyone on the project, there was not an increase of folks "on the bench." Rather, the percentage of direct time being charged decreased and the indirect percentage increased. It doesn't take a large swing in this percentage to affect your indirect budget if the change affects a large enough number of people. However, a traditional bench report will not predict this increase in indirect spending. This is why consulting businesses plan by creating and tracking the direct/indirect percentage for everyone in the organization. It is more difficult to see at a glance what the effect of a change will be on your budget. When Touchstone ran into a funding issue one quarter, I was still using the traditional bench report to estimate indirect costs. The early warning signs of an indirect problem were not as visible to me, and therefore I didn't implement the necessary mitigation steps needed to avert a problem. Had I realized that the business models were different, I would have altered the monthly reports that I relied on to manage the company. With the proper reports, I could have better planned for a downturn in the Touchstone business and taken steps to mitigate the effect on SRA's margin.

Prior to closing an acquisition, ensure that you understand the business model of the acquired company, and ensure that the appropriate management controls are in place.

57. Why did you buy them?

The single reason that most integrations fail is that the folks responsible for ensuring that an acquisition is successful do not understand the reasons that the company decided to make the acquisition. The folks responsible for the acquisition understand the value of the acquired company, but that value did not become a part of the integration strategy.

When you decide to acquire a company, you have to ask, "What are its strengths?" Use that answer to guide the integration. Sometimes the strengths will be in the managers, sometimes in the customer set, sometimes in the technology. Sometimes the strength of a company will not be obvious. That was the situation with Touchstone Consulting.

Touchstone was a management consulting company that performed work for the government and had customers within both Defense and civil government. We weren't sure what to do with Touchstone when we acquired it. Should we integrate it into our civil sector where most of our consulting services resided, or into our defense sector where a lot of their growth was projected? Or should we break it up to fit into our corporate structure? We couldn't answer this question when we first acquired the firm, so we left it alone as a separate business unit reporting to me, the COO, directly. At first we didn't understand that the real value in Touchstone was that the government viewed it as an independent consultant and evaluator of programs. A large part of its value was in its image as being independent of any government contractor. Leaving it as a separate business unit and allowing it to continue the use of the Touchstone name in some form is what enabled its value to continue. The right integration approach for Touchstone was to leave it separate and not integrate it into an existing business unit.

There are many examples of where SRA got this right, and we did achieve the synergy and value we expected. The acquisitions of Orion Scientific Systems and Adroit Systems Inc. are two examples where SRA kept a focus on the value of the acquired company and why it purchased that company. Orion was acquired to help SRA built a practice in counterterrorism and counterintelligence, homeland security, and law enforcement. Orion also brought some software products and tools that helped differentiate it from competitors in these areas. Adroit was acquired for its work in C4ISR and Unmanned Aerial Vehicles (UAVs). The Departments of Defense and Homeland Security were beginning to emphasize these areas. In both these cases, SRA was able to take a business with revenue below $30M and more than triple that revenue within a few years. SRA was able to accomplish this growth by staying true to the value of the acquisition. In both cases, SRA let the senior staff do what they do best even as the acquired company was being integrated into SRA. SRA was able to build and grow a business around those acquisitions using the acquired company to form the core of the new business.

In many cases, the most important value of a company is its people. Unfortunately, a common situation for an acquiring company is not to know what to do with the leaders of the new company. All too often, the culture of the acquiring company doesn't give a full voice to those new leaders, nor has the acquiring company figured out how to fit new senior people into the company. In any acquisition, it is the best people who leave first. If you have acquired companies and didn't realize the benefits that you expected, ask first how many of the leaders from the acquired company are still with you a year or two later. If the answer is that a lot of them left, then you have the answer to why the acquisition didn't work out. You have to have figured out how to use the leaders from a company before the acquisition is complete.

You need to understand the real value of a company early. Waiting until after the closing is too late. The next rule will offer a way to ensure that that value remains the focus of integration.

58. Integration starts at due diligence

Many companies will claim that they follow this rule, but they don't know how to make it real. A common practice in larger companies is to run the due diligence out of a separate corporate development staff. The work of the due diligence staff is complete once the acquisition closes. The process of integration is then left to a separate division, usually a business unit that had some, but not necessarily the bulk of, the due diligence responsibility. In these cases, even if the business unit gets involved before the acquisition is complete, there is still a division of labor between the corporate staff and the business unit in due diligence activities. I've even seen some acquisitions where the business unit had minimal involvement in the details of due diligence.

We took a different approach at SRA. Even after we became a large company, we approached due diligence like a small company. We formed a due diligence team that was constituted from subject matter experts from across the company. This team contained folks from both the business unit and corporate staff. We operated as one team with regular meetings, usually weekly, and one consolidated action item list that we reviewed and discussed as a team. The same team stayed involved during the integration phase. During due diligence, we were able to identify those areas that could become problematic during integration, and we were able to tailor our integration plan for that area early. In this way, all the interested parties had a role in developing a tailored integration plan and seeing it through to completion.

59. Faster is better

The one question that always comes up when discussing the integration of acquisitions is "How fast should we integrate?" While there is no single answer that fits every situation, in general, faster is better. However, this rule does need to be modified in some situations. It is worthwhile to consider this question from several perspectives: the external image, internal company systems, employees, and customers.

Many companies, especially the large ones, appear to integrate new acquisitions immediately upon the close of the transaction. Overnight, they change the signs in front of the company's buildings, they change the website, and maybe even change email accounts of the staff. There are a lot of advantages to this approach. It makes it clear to the world that the two companies are now operating as one. At least to the outside world, it can look as if the company is starting to achieve real synergy from the acquisition. Making these changes quickly does, of course, require a lot of early preparation. When you can afford to do this preparation, this is usually the best approach for branding.

The only times where I would not recommend a fast approach occur when one of the key reasons that you are acquiring the company is for the brand value of its name or there is value to the acquired company's retaining its independence. I described this case in Rule 57 when I discussed the value of keeping Touchstone independent.

Many companies that change the name of the acquired company overnight do not change the internal business systems of that company. They let the acquired company operate with its own financial and HR systems and even maintain many of its systems for project management. This is very inefficient. It is difficult and costly to transition the internal systems, but the faster you can change these, the sooner you will be able to achieve the benefits of the acquisition. At SRA, we were great believers in the efficiencies of a central services model for back-office functions. Even with a company that has a different business model, as I described with Touchstone, it pays to transition the financial and other systems quickly. With Touchstone, I assigned a senior person, Wayne Blackburn, to work with the Touchstone financial people and managers to prepare financial reports in our standard format. This began immediately after integration, even before we were able to migrate their financials to our system. Since Wayne and I had worked together for many years, he knew precisely what was expected of a business unit and was able to train the Touchstone staff. It is important that you allocate sufficient resources to train the acquired staff in how you want to operate and to assign the role of trainer to a senior person on your staff.

I can't emphasize enough the importance of quickly explaining the acquisition to all the employees of an acquired company. The faster that the reason for the acquisition is clear to employees, the sooner they will accept the acquisition and get on with their work. Otherwise, the acquisition will be a source of discussion that absorbs time and energy. The day that we announced the acquisition of Galaxy Corporation, we held a video teleconference with all Galaxy employees. Galaxy was a $100M company with three major offices and employees at other locations. The three major offices were connected via video conference and the remote employees were connected via teleconference. We had a senior person from SRA at each of the major locations. We discussed the rationale for the acquisition, how Galaxy employees fit into the SRA vision, our plans for the acquisition process and what it meant to each employee and the customers, how we intended to communicate progress in integrating Galaxy's benefits and systems, and they could ask questions after that day's session.

It is also important to rapidly convey the values of your company and explain clearly what is expected of each employee. When we acquired Touchstone, I led a one-and-a-half-hour session on SRA's values. It was probably the first time that most of the employees were exposed to such an in-depth discussion of corporate values. I did this within the first month following the acquisition.

It is important that you quickly explain the acquisition to customers. The customers of an acquired company need to be reassured that the acquisition does not present any risk to the performance of their projects. You need to meet with these customers, reassure them that projects have management attention, that the people on those projects will be taken care of, and that you will pay particular attention to those projects.

Soon after we acquired Galaxy, I met with a customer of that firm who asked me why the Galaxy people didn't have new SRA business cards. We thought it was a good idea to slowly transition the Galaxy name, but that approach was confusing to customers. Faster would have been better.

There is one area where it might be better to go slow, where faster is not better. It might not be a good idea to transition an acquired company's bonus program immediately. In general, companies that I've known do a good job of transitioning benefit programs in a way that keeps people whole when their benefits are taken together. That is, when looking at everything, vacation time, 401(k) match, health benefits, etc., you can generally adjust salaries or benefits so that most employees are not disadvantaged. You might need to give some folks a small salary increase to compensate, but this is usually small, and I've found that these changes are easily explained and accepted by most employees. It is usually not that easy to deal with the bonus program.

Most of the small businesses that we've looked to acquire offered bonuses to a much larger percentage of the staff than we typically did. This was true not just at SRA, but at every other company where I've helped with acquisitions. In some companies, most everyone received an annual bonus of some amount. That isn't a good idea for a company of any size, but a large business just can't afford to do that. The bonus pool in every company is limited, and it should go to those outstanding performers who most helped the company achieve its goals. Nevertheless, many small business owners have a different approach. A common means of dealing with this situation after an acquisition is to eliminate bonuses for many people and increase salaries by an amount equal to their average bonus. People will like the salary increase, but come the end of the year, they will still expect a bonus. You don't want to do anything to demotivate new employees. There is a way to avoid some of the negative effects of eliminating bonuses. Create a transition plan that reduces and eliminates bonuses over time. This can work a couple of different ways. Let's say that in an acquired company, 80 percent of the employees have been getting bonuses, but in your company only 30 percent of employees typically get an annual bonus. Instead of 80 percent of the employees getting a bonus, in the first year 65 percent get a bonus. The second year, 45 percent get a bonus, and the third year 30 percent. You can handle the 40 percent who don't get a bonus the first year with a salary increase, or simply don't give a bonus to new employees who don't expect one, but keep the better performers on a bonus plan. This approach work best if the acquired company remains largely intact during the transition period.

Whatever approach you take, you have to have your detailed plan established before you close so it can be explained clearly to all new employees.

60. Address the hidden people issues

Dealing with the people issues is the hardest part of integration. Companies are usually good dealing with the obvious problems such as merging the benefit programs. Most of the issues with an acquisition are not that obvious. You need a mechanism for discovering the hidden problems that the acquisition has created.

We found that many of these problems can be avoided with a simple technique: put an HR generalist physically on-site with the acquired company at least two or three days a week for several months. Put a good listener in this role. When we did this, there was a steady stream of people going into their office to discuss their personal situations. At first folks talked mainly about questions or issues with their health benefits. Almost everyone has some question about how the changes in benefits affects him. After a while, folks opened up about how they felt about a lot of topics. These HR folks became the face of the integration to many people. They discovered how the average worker and the customers felt about the acquisition. As senior managers, we had a degree of visibility into what employees really felt that we never would have had. We received early warning signs of employee issues before they became major issues, and we still had time to fix them. These HR generalists helped smooth over a lot of potential issues.

61. Acquire adjacencies

Barry Landew and Kevin Robbins emphasized this rule to me. Barry and Kevin were responsible for acquisitions at SRA while I was the COO. They now lead the consulting company Wolf Den Associates.

One of the reasons why acquisitions fail is that companies acquire other companies who are too similar or too dissimilar to their current work. The more an acquired company overlaps with your current projects, the more issues you will have with territorial conflicts. On the other hand, if the acquired company has skills and customers that are very much different from your current work, you may not have the skills and knowledge to properly manage that business or be able to develop a vision for your combined company that drives your future strategy.

You want to acquire companies that are adjacent to your current work. This adjacency can be either adjacent new skills or adjacent new customers. The acquired company should add something new to your portfolio of projects or skills, but not be so different so as to substantially change your vision. You need to have some idea as to how your acquisitions will fit into your brand. One of the reasons why the Orion and Adroit acquisitions were so successful is that they were in the perfect adjacent space. They brought new customers and capabilities, but they were not so far from SRA's core skills as to make strange bedfellows. They were experts in fields that were a natural for SRA expansion, and it was just faster and cheaper to acquire these skills rather than develop them in-house.

The acquisition of Spectrum Corporation is another example of acquiring adjacent, needed skills. Implementing ERP systems became the primary means of the government's building some new business systems. SRA had been watching the ERP phenomenon, but had not yet gotten into that market. We knew that we needed to have these skills if we were to stay a player in systems development. It would have been time-consuming for us to build those skills and experience by hiring and training ERP professionals. We did try a few approaches to bidding ERP projects. We did train some staff and bid a few jobs without success. It became clear that the fastest way to build an ERP practice was to acquire one. Spectrum had excellent past performance and respected people. Their customers were the same government customers that we knew, but their skills were adjacent, while different from ours. We had expertise in custom system development. They had expertise in system development using ERPs. In addition, they fit perfectly into our vision and strategy of being one of the leading government systems integrators. Acquiring adjacent skills in a new technology is one of the criteria that could help ensure a successful acquisition.

Acquiring companies without thinking through how they will fit into your vision could have an unexpected negative affect later. There may come a time when circumstances are right for you to sell your company, or perhaps you just want to attract outside investors. An acquiring company or investor will need to understand your vision and focus. Without a clear focus, it will be more difficult to attract interested parties. We faced this issue when we were interested in selling TechTeam Government Solutions Inc. TechTeam Government was formed through four acquisitions. While all four companies provided professional services to the government, they were very different from one another. Some of the work was long-term information technology network support work for the Department of Defense. One of the component companies focused on health-related IT projects. Yet another part of the business performed high-end analytical support on short-term projects. This part of the business had a business model similar to that of a commercial consulting business—short-term projects with everyone working at least some time on direct projects and some time on indirect corporate research projects. A unifying principle that tied these four businesses together was not obvious.

We hadn't intended to sell TechTeam. Our plans when I joined were to make additional acquisitions and continue to grow the business. However, when the stock market crashed toward the end of 2008, we realized that we couldn't raise money for additional acquisitions, and our investors (TechTeam was a publicly traded company) decided that it was financially better to sell the business. Several of the large companies that looked at us couldn't figure out how to integrate us into their business. They would have to split us up. Our health business would have to be put with their health business, our DoD business moved into their DoD business, etc. That was just not an attractive integration approach for most companies.

Many companies who are interested in acquiring other companies will have ideas of the type of business they want to acquire and may keep the adjacency rule in mind. There is, however, another facet to looking for companies adjacent to yours, and that is to look for companies whose culture is close to yours. This may not be as obvious or as easy as you might think. I was recently advising a company that was looking to acquire a company in Huntsville, Alabama, since it saw that geographic area as a growing market. One of the companies that we met with told us that it contributed 10 percent of everyone's salary to each person's 401(k) account. The firm made this contribution regardless of the amount of the employee's contribution. The management of the company said that they wanted to maintain that practice after the acquisition. We didn't see any way to make that work, since that practice was very different from what we were doing with current employees. This extreme amount of match might also be a sign that there was more of a culture of entitlement than we could tolerate. We decided very quickly to not pursue that company.

If you acquire companies whose business is not adjacent but is far removed from your business, then it is even more likely that its people are used to being treated differently. Cultures may be very different. Salary scales and bonus philosophies may be very different and difficult to reconcile. Organizational principles may be different. Even hiring criteria may be different. A product company, for example, may hire for innovative thinking, while a service business will hire people who care about customer service. You need to recognize early when integrating companies would be too difficult.

At SRA, cultural compatibility was a major criterion in selecting acquisition candidates. You will not find another company with the same culture as yours, but the cultures need to be close and compatible. This is another form of adjacency that you need to consider.

PART SIX
UNIFYING CONCEPTS

Tying it all together

Many of the rules in this book can be derived from three principles: (1) Take care of your customers. (2) Take care of your people. (3) Manage your company well. The reason for taking care of your customers is obvious. They are the reason that you are in business. A lot of companies recognize this. Taking care of your people comes next. Most of the assets in a service business go home every night. Most companies understand these two principles. It is in the application of the third principle that they go awry. It is crucial to understand how to apply all three principles.

1. Take care of your customers. Taking care of your customer means that you act in its best interest all the time, even when it appears to not be in your company's best interest. You act in the customer's best interest even it means that you will be embarrassed or lose money.

When I visit with a customer, I like to hear the people say that our folks are doing a great job. Sometimes a customer's executive would say to me, "Your people are giving me advice that is not in your best interest." That was the best thing I could hear. That meant that our folks understood that if they acted in the customer's best interest, SRA would benefit eventually. Sometimes one of our project managers would tell me that for an upcoming task, he knew that the customer had, say, $200,000 but that we could do the task for $130,000 and still make a fair profit. What should we propose? I would always say, Tell the customer that we could do that task for $130,000. What do you think they are going to do with the other $70,000? They are not going to return it to the U.S. Treasury. Chances are that they have some other tasks that they want done but they don't think they have the money for them. With this "extra" money, they will probably ask us to do something else that they want done.

One way that I've explained this principle comes from SRA's Vision Statement. SRA's vision includes the statement that SRA creates value for its customers. What does it mean to "create value"? Folks understand the concept of providing value to your customers, but creating value goes further. A company creates value when the product or services it provides is worth more to a customer than what the customer pays for them. For example, if you buy a book for $25, if that book is worth more to you than $25, then that author and publisher have created value. If a customer pays us $100,000 or $1M, the value of the services we provide have to be worth more **to the customer** than what it is paying. In monthly project reviews, some of our managers required that their PM tell them how they created value for their customer that month. They required their PMs to tell them how they did more than just doing what they were asked. How did they really make their customer look good to *its* customers?

I found that we already had one way to measure our performance against this principle. As I described in Rule 6, on our customer satisfaction survey we asked the question, "Are we proposing innovative solutions?" While not every project required innovation, our customers understood this question to mean, "Were we going beyond the minimum of what we had to do to make them successful? Were we making suggestions on how to improve their operation?" I found that the answers to this question correlated with winning (or losing) our recompetes. Too often I heard a project manager being characterized as being a good PM: "He does everything our customer asks him to do." That is just not enough in this competitive environment. That is how good companies lose their work. Our customer's work is changing at a very fast rate. Technology is changing, budgets are changing, and the expectations of our customer are changing. Our project teams have to help their customers change with the times, otherwise they will select another contractor. Earlier I pointed out why good proposals don't invariably win. Likewise, good work isn't necessarily sufficient to win recompetes. You have to create real value for your customer.

2. Take care of your employees. The service business is a people business, so it makes sense to take care of your employees. They are your most valuable asset. You need to manage in a way that enables people to succeed. All too often, company cultures and processes make it difficult for people to succeed. When processes rather than common sense drive behavior, you need to rethink which processes have to be absolutely followed for legal reasons, and which processes should be considered guidance. Train your people well, and trust them to take care of their customers. Reward and recognize them for taking care of their customers. These two principles complement each other.

3. Manage your company well. Managing your company well means using business judgment and common sense to make decisions. Many managers manage to financial metrics such as profit and revenue. These are important trailing indicators, but they are not metrics that should guide your management decisions.

You should manage to leading indicators. Leading indicators are metrics that are useful in predicting how well you will do in the future. Examples of leading indicators are: backlog, change in backlog, pipeline size, win rate, the ratio of new wins to the rate at which you are executing current work, and the rate of turnover. Gross and net income are important metrics, but, as trailing indicators, they are a scorecard on how well you made business decisions. If you are managing to these trailing indicators, then chances are that you are trying to dig yourself out of a hole you didn't want to be in.

Managing your company well also means that you will make sure everyone understands that the *reason you are in business* is to deliver a product or service to customers. Many people think that the reason that you are in business is to make money. Of course you have to make a profit or you will go out of business. But that is not the REASON you are in business. Think about it in terms of your own life and who you want to do business with. Would you rather choose a dry cleaner who believes that he wants to give you the best dry cleaning service possible, or a dry cleaner who is only interested in making money and the service he delivers to you is secondary? That second dry cleaner will likely go out of business in a short time. If you stay committed to creating real value for your customers, you are on the right path to growth and success.

In order to successfully grow a business you need to do everything well. These three principles and the 61 rules are designed to help you achieve your goals.

Glossary

AWIS: Army World Wide Military Command and Control System Information System. SRA's first large project was to develop the requirements for this system.

Backlog: Unfilled orders. A contractor might receive, for example, a contract for $5M of services over five years, that is, $1M a year for five years. After one year, they would have $4M left in backlog.

Bid: A proposal. Bid can also be used as a verb meaning "to prepare and submit a proposal."

Black Hat Review: A competitive assessment to address the strengths and weaknesses of the competition against the evaluation criteria and against your strengths and weaknesses.

Blanket Purchase Agreement (BPA): A simplified acquisition approach that a government agency can set up for repetitive purchases. This simplifies the ordering process in return for discounted rates.

C4ISR: Command, Control, Communications, Computers, Intelligence, Surveillance and Reconnaissance. Adding Surveillance and Reconnaissance qualifications to SRA's existing work was a key reason for acquiring Adroit Systems, Inc.

Capability Maturity Model: The government funded Carnegie Mellon University to establish a Software Engineering Institute (SEI). The SEI developed a five-stage model of the maturity of the process that a company uses to develop software.

CIO: Chief Information Officer (CIO) or Information Technology (IT) Director, is a title given to the most senior executive in a government agency responsible for the information technology and computer systems. Each government agency is required to have a CIO responsible for all of the agency's information technology needs.

Cloud Computing Services: Cloud computing, in this context, refers to hosting of a government software application on computers owned and operated by a commercial firm at a non-government facility. The government has established rigorous policies and procedures for approving providers of this service.

Commercial-off-the-shelf (COTS): An item that is not developed for the government and is available to the general public.

Configuration Control Board (CCB): Also called a "Change Control Board" is a group that evaluates and approves or disapproves of proposed changes to a system.

Cost-reimbursable contract: A type of contract where the government agrees to pay the contractor the actual costs of performing the service plus an agreed upon fee.

COTR: Contracting Officer's Technical Representative. This is the government person who usually oversees the day-to-day work of a contractor.

Customer Relationship Management (CRM): CRM refers to a strategy or methodology that helps an enterprise manage its relationships with its customers. Government organizations that provide service to other government organizations adopted these principles, and some agencies bought and used commercial CRM software products to support these principles.

Debrief: At the conclusion of an acquisition after the government has selected a winner, it presents the reasons for its decision to the companies that bid on the job.

Deficiency request: A part of the government acquisition process. After reviewing proposals, the government may inform the bidders as to where their proposal does not meet the requirements listed in the RFP. The government may choose to send deficiency requests to the bidders, but they do not have to.

DISA: Defense Information Systems Agency

Discriminator: A characteristic or feature of a proposal that offers a unique benefit to the customer. Every proposal should contain several discriminators that support the customer selecting that proposal over the others that are submitted.

Due diligence: The process through which a potential acquirer evaluates a target company for an acquisition.

ECP: Engineering change proposal. After a contract is awarded, any changes to the requirements must be reflected in the contract. The ECP is the documentation of the required changes and their effect on the contract.

ERP: Enterprise resource planning. A commercial software system that is used to manage the information and functions of a business. These systems may manage a portion of a business such as finance or human resources or they may be used to integrate several functions into one system. Government agencies, including the Department of Defense, use ERP systems for many of their business processes including finance and human resources.

GS-11, GS-12: The General Schedule (GS) is the predominant pay scale within the United States Civil Service. The GS includes the majority of white collar (professional, technical, administrative, and clerical) positions. The scale goes from GS-1 through GS-15.

GWAC: Government-Wide Acquisition Contract. Some contracts can be used by any organization within in the government. These contracts are called "GWACs."

ID/IQ: Indefinite Delivery/Indefinite Quantity. This is a type of contract that provides for an indefinite quantity of supplies or services during a fixed period of time.

IRS: Internal Revenue Service

IT: Information Technology

LPTA: Low Price, Technically Acceptable. An LPTA acquisition is one where the winner is the company that offers the lowest price while meeting the minimally acceptable requirements. This is in contrast to a "Best Value" procurement where the government may select a higher priced offer that offers additional value above and beyond the minimum requirements.

Leading indicator: A metric that can be used to predict future results or trends. Pipeline, change in pipeline, and win rate are all leading indicators.

NIH: National Institutes of Health

NGB: National Guard Bureau

Object Oriented: A technique for designing and writing computer programs where the program is organized as a collection of interacting objects rather than a list of tasks to perform.

Outsourcing: The contracting out of an internal business process to a third-party organization.

Paradigm shift: A profound change in a fundamental model or perception of events. In the contracting of technology by the government, this refers to major changes in technology and major shifts in how the government buys services.

PEO: Program Executive Officer. A PEO is one of the few key individuals within the Department of Defense with authority to acquire major systems.

PEO STAMIS: The PEO for Standard Army Information Systems.

Pipeline: A list of potential opportunities on which a company is likely to submit a bid.

PM: Program or Project Manager

Prime contractor: Most government contracts are issued to a team of contractors. The lead contractor is the "Prime" contractor who then employs subcontractors. The word "prime" is sometimes used as shorthand for "prime contractor" or as a verb meaning "to bid a contract as the prime contractor."

RCAS: Reserve Component Automation System. This was one of SRA's first jobs that had a value over $100M.

RFP: Request for Proposals. A request for proposal (RFP) is a solicitation made, through a bidding process, by an agency interested in the procurement of a service, system, or product. Sometimes this will be issued as a Request for Quotes (RFQ).

Recompete: The government frequently issues a contract for a base period, usually a year, with options to extend the contract for a specified number of additional years. A base year with four option years is frequently the specified period. At the end of the contract, the government will then issue a new RFP and hold a new competition. This new competition is a recompetition of the work. Recompetes are also called "rebids."

Red Team Review: An internal final review of the draft of a proposal to predict how the customer will score the proposal and to identify ways to improve the proposal's score.

SES: Senior Executive Service. A position classification, for senior civilians working in either the Department of Defense or civil government, that is somewhat analogous to general or admiral.

Sub: Subcontractor. A company that is on a team providing services through a prime contractor. Subcontractors do not have a contract directly with the government. Their contract is with the prime contractor only.

Sustaining Base Information System: An Army system for supporting the activities of an installation in the United States. For example, the software supports the registration of new soldiers as they move onto the base.

Task order: A task order is the means by which the government buys a service under an existing ID/IQ contract.

Trailing indicator: A metric that describes past performance. Revenue and profit are examples of trailing indicators.

Web portal: A Web page that offers a broad array of resources or services.

Win Rate: This can be either the ratio of the number of jobs won to the number of jobs bid or the dollar amount of jobs won to the dollar amount of jobs bid.

Index

Index

About the Author

David Kriegman has spent 30 years growing and managing companies that provide professional services to the government.

At SRA International, Mr. Kriegman served in many leadership roles from project manager to chief operating officer during a time when SRA grew from $5M in annual revenue to over $1B. Before becoming SRA's COO, Mr. Kriegman was the director of Defense Systems; he grew that business from $48M to over $400M in seven years. While he was an executive at SRA, the company was recognized seven times by Fortune magazine as one of the 100 Best Companies to Work For. When he was COO, SRA was recognized by Washingtonian magazine as one the best places to work in the D.C. area.

After leaving SRA, Mr. Kriegman became president of a venture capital-backed start-up and later served as president of a company formed through multiple acquisitions. Mr. Kriegman's acquisition experience covers both buying and selling companies.

Currently Mr. Kriegman serves as CEO of Z2B, LLC, a firm established to help other companies achieve their strategic growth goals. His current clients include companies of all sizes, from start-ups to established public companies with revenue of over $2B. In addition to his consulting and speaking activities, Mr.Kriegman serves on the board of several companies.

Mr. Kriegman can be reached at www.Z2B-LLC.com